W9-BSI-850

DK Travel Guides

SPANISH
PHRASE BOOK

A Dorling Kindersley Book

Dorling Kindersley

LONDON, NEW YORK, SYDNEY, DELHI, PARIS,
MUNICH and JOHANNESBURG

www.dk.com

Compiled by Lexus Ltd with
Alicia de Benito de Harland and Mike Harland

Published in the United States by Dorling Kindersley Publishing, Inc.
95 Madison Avenue, New York, New York 10016

First American Edition 1998
Reprinted with corrections 2000
2 4 6 8 10 9 7 5 3 1

Dorling Kindersley books can be purchased in bulk quantities at discounted
prices for use in promotions or as premiums. We are also able to offer special
editions and personalized jackets, corporate imprints, and excerpts from all of
our books, tailored specifically to meet your own needs. To find out more, please
contact: Special Markets Department, Dorling Kindersley Publishing, Inc.,
95 Madison Avenue, New York, NY 10016; Fax: 800-600-9098.

Library of Congress Cataloging-in-Publication Data
Spanish phrase book. -- 1st American ed.
    p.   cm. -- (Dorling Kindersley travel guide phrase books)
English and Spanish.
Includes index.
ISBN 0-7894-3233-1 (alk. paper)
1. Spanish language--Conversation and phrase books--
English.   I. DK Publishing. Inc.   II. Series.
PC4121.S6765   1998
468.3'421--DC21   97-47228
                                                              CIP

Picture Credits

Jacket: all special photography Max Alexander, Joe Cornish, Steve Gorton,
Dave King, Neil Lucas, Neil Mersh, and Linda Whitwam.

Printed and bound in Italy by Printer Trento Srl.

CONTENTS

PREFACE

This *Dorling Kindersley Travel Guides Phrase Book* has been compiled by experts to meet the general needs of tourists and business travelers. Arranged under headings such as Hotels, Driving, and so forth, the ample selection of useful words and phrases is supported by a 2,000-line mini-dictionary. There is also an extensive menu guide listing approximately 600 dishes or methods of cooking and presentation.

Typical replies to questions you may ask during your trip, and the signs or instructions you may see or hear, are shown in tinted boxes. In the main text, the pronunciation of Spanish words and phrases is imitated in English sound syllables. The Introduction provides guidelines to Spanish pronunciation.

Dorling Kindersley Travel Guides are recognized as the world's best travel guides. Each title features specially commissioned color photographs, cutaways of major buildings, 3-D aerial views, and detailed maps, plus information on sights, events, hotels, restaurants, shopping, and entertainment.

Dorling Kindersley Travel Guides titles include:
Spain · Barcelona · Madrid · Seville & Andalusia · Amsterdam
Australia · Sydney · Berlin · Budapest · California · Florida
Hawaii · New York · San Francisco & Northern California · Canada
France · Loire Valley · Paris · Provence · Great Britain · London
Ireland · Dublin · Scotland · Greece: Athens & the Mainland
The Greek Islands · Istanbul · Italy · Florence & Tuscany
Milan & the Lakes · Naples · Rome · Sardinia · Sicily
Venice & the Veneto · Jerusalem & the Holy Land · Mexico
Moscow · St Petersburg · Portugal · Lisbon · Prague
South Africa · Thailand · Vienna · Warsaw

INTRODUCTION

Pronunciation

When reading the imitated pronunciation, stress the part that is underlined. Pronounce each syllable as if it formed part of an English word and you will be understood sufficiently well. Remember the points below and your pronunciation will be even closer to the correct Spanish.

g	always hard as in "get"
H	represents the guttural sound of "ch"
I	pronounced as "eye"
ow	as in "cow"
s	always sound the Spanish "s" as a double "ss" as in "missing," *never* like the "s" in "easy"
th	as in "thin," *not* as in "they"
y	always as in "yet," *not* as in "eye" (e.g. **bien** *byen*, **siento** *syentoh*)

Don't be worried by the varying pronunciations you are certain to hear in some parts of Spain. An example is the sounding of "z" (and of "c" before e or i) like an English "s"—in this instance we recommend that you don't copy it, but lisp the sound as we have imitated it. Similarly, in certain circumstances, the Spanish "v" can be pronounced as either a "v" or a "b," so that **vaca** sounds like "baca."

Genders and Articles

Spanish has two genders for nouns—masculine and feminine. In this book, we generally give the definite article ("the")—**el** for masculine nouns, **la** for feminine nouns, **los** for masculine plural nouns, and **las** for feminine plural nouns. Where the indefinite article ("a, an") is more appropriate, we have given **un** for masculine nouns and **una** for feminine nouns, or the words for "some"—**unos** (masculine) and **unas** (feminine).

USEFUL EVERYDAY PHRASES

YES, NO, OK, ETC.

Yes/No
Sí/No
see/noh

Excellent!
¡Estupendo!
estoopendoh

Don't!
¡No!
noh

OK
Vale
baleh

That's fine
Está bien
esta byen

That's right
Eso es
essoh ess

GREETINGS, INTRODUCTIONS

How do you do? Pleased to meet you
¿Qué tal?, mucho gusto
keh tal, mootchoh goostoh

Good morning/good evening/good night
Buenos días/buenas tardes/buenas noches
bweh-noss dee-ass/bweh-nass tardess/bweh-nass notchess

Goodbye/Bye
Adiós
ad-yoss

How are you? *(familiar)*
¿Cómo está usted?   ¿Cómo estás?
koh-moh esta oosteh   *koh-moh estass*

My name is …
Me llamo …
meh yah-moh

What's your name? *(familiar)*
¿Cómo se llama usted?   ¿Cómo te llamas?
koh-moh seh yah-ma oosteh   *koh-moh teh yah-mass*

What's his/her name?
¿Cómo se llama él/ella?
koh-moh seh yah-ma el/eh-ya

May I introduce …?
Le presento a …
leh presentoh a

This is … *(introducing a man/woman)*
Éste/ésta es …
esteh/esta ess

Hello/Hi!
¡Hola!
oh-la

See you later!
¡Hasta luego!
asta lweh-goh

It's been nice meeting you *(to a man/woman)*
Mucho gusto en conocerle/conocerla
mootchoh goostoh en konoh-thairleh/konoh-thairla

PLEASE, THANK YOU, APOLOGIES

Thank you/No, thank you
Gracias/No, gracias
grath-yass/noh grath-yass

Please
Por favor
por fa-vor

Excuse me! *(when sneezing, etc.)*
¡Perdón!
pair-don

Sorry!
¡Perdón!/Lo siento
pair-don/loh syentoh

I'm really sorry
Lo siento muchísimo
loh syentoh mootchee-seemoh

It was/wasn't my fault
Ha sido/no ha sido culpa mía
a seedoh/noh a seedoh koolpa mee-a

WHERE, HOW, ASKING

Excuse me, please *(to get past)*
¿Me hace el favor?
meh ah-theh el fa-vor

Can you tell me …?
¿Puede decirme …?
pweh-deh detheer-meh

Can I have …?
¿Me da …?
meh da

Would you like a …?   *(familiar)*
¿Quiere un/una …?   ¿Quieres un/una …?
kyeh-reh oon/oona

Would you like to …?   *(familiar)*
¿Le gustaría …?   ¿Te gustaría …?
leh goostaree-a

Is there … here?
¿Hay … aquí?
I … akee

What's that?
¿Qué es eso?
keh ess esso

Where can I get …?
¿Dónde puedo conseguir …?
dondeh pweh-doh konseh-geer

How much is it?
¿Cuánto es?
kwantoh ess

Where is the …?
¿Dónde está el/la …?
dondeh esta el/la

Where are the restrooms?
¿Dónde están los servicios?
dondeh estan loss sair-veeth-yoss

Is there wheelchair access?
¿Hay acceso para sillas de ruedas?
I akthesoh a parra seeyahs de rooedas

Are there facilities for the disabled?
¿Hay acceso a minusváli dos?
I akthesoh a meenoosvalee dos

ABOUT ONESELF

I'm from …
Soy de …
soy deh

I'm … years old
Tengo … años
teng-goh … ahn-yoss

I'm a …
Soy …
soy

I'm married/divorced
Estoy casado/divorciado
estoy kasadoh/deevorss-yah-doh

I'm single
Soy soltero
soy soltairoh

I have … sisters/brothers/children
Tengo … hermanas/hermanos/hijos
teng-goh … airmah-nass/airmah-noss/ee-Hoss

LIKES, DISLIKES, SOCIALIZING

I like/love …
Me gusta/encanta el/la …
meh goosta/enkanta el/la

I like/love swimming/traveling
Me gusta/encanta nadar/viajar
meh goosta/enkanta nadar/vya-Har

I don't like …
No me gusta el/la …
noh meh goosta el/la

I don't like swimming/traveling
No me gusta nadar/viajar
noh meh goosta nadar/vya-Har

I hate …
Detesto …
detestoh

Do you like …?
¿Le gusta …?
leh goosta

It's delicious/awful!
¡Es delicioso/horrible!
ess deleeth-yohsoh/orreebleh

I don't drink/smoke
No bebo/fumo
noh beboh/foomoh

Do you mind if I smoke?
¿Le importa que fume?
leh eemporta keh foomeh

I don't eat meat or fish
No como carne ni pescado
noh koh-moh karneh nee peskadoh

What would you like (to drink)?
¿Qué quiere (beber/tomar)?
keh kyeh-reh bebair/tomar

I would like a …
Quería …
keh-ree-a

Nothing for me, thanks
No quiero nada, gracias
noh kyeh-roh nada grath-yass

I'll get this one
Ahora invito yo
a-ora eembeetoh yoh

Cheers! *(toast)*
¡Salud!
saloo

I would like to …
Quería …
keh-ree-a

Let's go to Seville/the movies
Vamos a Sevilla/al cine
vamoss a sevee-ya/al theeneh

Let's go swimming/for a walk
Vamos a nadar/a dar un paseo
vamoss a nadar/a dar oon passeh-oh

What's the weather like?
¿Qué tiempo hace?
keh tyempoh ah-theh

The weather's awful
Hace un tiempo malísimo
ah-theh oon tyempoh maleesseemoh

It's pouring down
Está lloviendo a cántaros
esta yovyendoh a kant-ah-ross

It's really hot
Hace muchísimo calor
ah-theh mootcheesseemoh kalor

HELP, PROBLEMS

Can you help me?
¿Puede ayudarme?
pw<u>eh</u>-deh ayood<u>a</u>rmeh

I don't understand
No comprendo
noh kompr<u>e</u>ndoh

Do you speak English/French/German/?
¿Habla usted inglés/francés/alemán?
<u>ah</u>-bla oost<u>eh</u> eengl<u>e</u>ss/franth<u>e</u>ss/alleh-m<u>a</u>n

Does anyone here speak English?
¿Hay alguien aquí que hable inglés?
i <u>a</u>lgyen ak<u>ee</u> keh <u>ah</u>bleh eengl<u>e</u>ss

I can't speak Spanish
No hablo español
noh <u>ah</u>-bloh esspan-y<u>o</u>ll

I don't know
No sé
noh seh

What's wrong?
¿Qué pasa?
keh p<u>a</u>ssa

Please speak more slowly
Por favor, hable más despacio
por fa-v<u>o</u>r <u>ah</u>-bleh mass dessp<u>a</u>th-yoh

Please write it down for me
Por favor, escríbamelo
por fa-v<u>o</u>r eskr<u>ee</u>ba-meh-loh

I've lost my way
Me he perdido
meh eh pair<u>dee</u>doh

Go away!
¡Váyase!
vah-ya-seh

TALKING TO RECEPTIONISTS, ETC.

I have an appointment with …
Tengo una cita con …
t<u>e</u>ng-goh <u>oo</u>na th<u>ee</u>ta kon

I'd like to see …
Quisiera ver a …
keess-y<u>eh</u>-ra vair a

Here's my card
Aquí tiene mi tarjeta
ak<u>ee</u> ty<u>e</u>neh mee tar-н<u>eh</u>-ta

My company is …
Soy de la compañía …
soy deh la kompany<u>ee</u>-a

May I use your phone?
¿Puedo usar su teléfono?
pw<u>eh</u>-doh ooss<u>a</u>r soo teh-l<u>e</u>ffonoh

THINGS YOU'LL HEAR

¡adelante!	come in!
aquí tiene	here you are
¡bien!	good!
¡buen viaje!	have a good trip!
¿cómo?	excuse me?
¿cómo está usted?	how are you?

→

¿cómo le va?	how are things?
¡cuánto lo siento!	I'm so sorry!
¡cuidado!	look out!
de acuerdo	OK
de nada	you're welcome, don't mention it
¿de verdad?	is that right?
¡encantado!	pleased to meet you!
eso es	that's right
exactamente/exacto	exactly
gracias, igualmente	thank you, the same to you
¡hasta luego!	goodbye! see you later!
¡hola!	hello! hi!
muchas gracias	thank you very much
muy bien, gracias —¿y usted?	very well, thank you —and you?
no comprendo	I don't understand
no sé	I don't know
por favor	please
¿qué ha dicho?	what did you say?
¿qué tal?, mucho gusto	how do you do? nice to meet you
sírvase usted mismo	help yourself

THINGS YOU'LL SEE

abierto	open
agua potable	drinking water
ascensor	elevator
aseos	restrooms
caballeros	men
caja	cashier, checkout, cash register
calle	street
carretera	road
cerrado (por vacaciones)	closed (for vacation period)

→

día festivo	national holiday
empujar	push
entrada	entrance
entrada gratuita/libre	admission free
entre sin llamar	enter without knocking
festivos	official holidays
horas de oficina	opening times
horas de visita	visiting hours
información turística	tourist information
laborables	working days
lavabos	restroom
ocupado	occupied
peligro	danger
planta baja	ground floor
precaución	caution
primer piso	second floor
privado	private
prohibido	prohibited, forbidden
recién pintado	wet paint
reservado	reserved
salida	exit
salida de emergencia	emergency exit
se alquila piso	apartment for rent
segundo piso	third floor
señoras	women's restroom
se prohíbe la entrada	no admittance
servicios	restroom
se vende	for sale
silencio	silence, quiet
sótano	basement
tirar	pull

COLLOQUIALISMS

You may hear these: to use some of them yourself could be risky!

emborra charse	to get drunk
a mares	a lot
¡anda ya!	get away! come off it!
cabrón	S.O.B.
cacharro	thing
¡cierra el pico!	shut your mouth!
¡no me vengas con esas!	you're kidding me!
de pacotilla	trashy
¡Dios mío!	my God!
¡me encanta qué maravilla!	that's really terrific!
¡estupendo!	wonderful!
¡genial!	great! fantastic!
ha sido una putada	it was a pain/nuisance
imbécil	imbecile
ir de copas	to go drinking
la mar de …	really/very …
lo digo de cachondeo	I'm only joking
¡maldita sea!	damn!
me está tomando el pelo	you're pulling my leg
¡ni de coña!	no way!
¡no me da la (real) gana!	I'm damned if I will!
putada	*(a general expression of annoyance)*
¡qué barbaridad!	no way!
¿qué hay?	how's things?
¡qué va!	no way!
tía	girl
tío	guy
¡vaya por Dios!	oh, dear!
¡váyase a paseo!	get lost!
¡vete a hacer puñetas!	get away!
ya está	there you are

DAYS, MONTHS, SEASONS

Sunday	domingo	*domeengoh*
Monday	lunes	*looness*
Tuesday	martes	*martess*
Wednesday	miércoles	*myairkoh-less*
Thursday	jueves	*Hweh-vess*
Friday	viernes	*vyairness*
Saturday	sábado	*sabbadoh*
January	enero	*enneh-roh*
February	febrero	*febreh-roh*
March	marzo	*marthoh*
April	abril	*abreel*
May	mayo	*mayyoh*
June	junio	*Hoon-yoh*
July	julio	*Hool-yoh*
August	agosto	*agostoh*
September	septiembre	*set-yembreh*
October	octubre	*oktoobreh*
November	noviembre	*nov-yembreh*
December	diciembre	*deeth-yembreh*
Spring	primavera	*preema-veh-ra*
Summer	verano	*verah-noh*
Fall	otoño	*oton-yoh*
Winter	invierno	*eemb-yairnoh*
Christmas	Navidad	*navee-da*
Christmas Eve	Nochebuena	*notcheh-bweh-na*
Easter	Pascua,	*paskwa,*
	Semana Santa	*semah-na santa*
Good Friday	Viernes Santo	*vyairness santoh*
New Year	Año Nuevo	*ahn-yoh nweh-voh*
New Year's Eve	Nochevieja	*notcheh-vyeh-Ha*

NUMBERS

0	cero *theh-roh*	10	diez *dyeth*
1	uno, una* *oonoh, oona*	11	once *ontheh*
2	dos *doss*	12	doce *doh-theh*
3	tres *tress*	13	trece *treh-theh*
4	cuatro *kwatroh*	14	catorce *katortheh*
5	cinco *theenkoh*	15	quince *keentheh*
6	seis *sayss*	16	dieciséis *dyeth-ee-sayss*
7	siete *see-eh-teh*	17	diecisiete *dyeth-ee-see-eh-teh*
8	ocho *otchoh*	18	dieciocho *dyeth-ee-otchoh*
9	nueve *nweh-veh*	19	diecinueve *dyeth-ee-nweh-veh*

20	veinte *vaynteh*
21	veintiuno *vayntee-oonoh*
22	veintidós *vayntee-doss*
30	treinta *traynta*
31	treinta y uno *trayntɪ oonoh*
32	treinta y dos *trayntɪ doss*
40	cuarenta *kwarenta*
50	cincuenta *theen-kwenta*
60	sesenta *sessenta*
70	setenta *setenta*
80	ochenta *otchenta*
90	noventa *noh-venta*
100	cien *thyen*
110	ciento diez *thyentoh dyeth*
200	doscientos, doscientas *doss-thyentoss, doss-thyentass*
500	quinientos, quinientas *keen-yentoss, keen-yentass*
700	setecientos, setecientas *seh-teh-thyentoss, seh-teh-thyentass*
1,000	mil *meel*
1,000,000	un millón *mee-yon*

* When **uno** precedes a masculine noun, it loses the final **o**, e.g. "1 point" is **un punto**. Feminine nouns take **una**, e.g. "1 peseta," **una peseta**. Numbers in the hundreds, 200, 300, etc., use the form ending in **-as** with feminine nouns, e.g. "300 notes," **trescientos billetes**; "500 pesetas," **quinientas pesetas**.

TIME

today	hoy	*oy*
yesterday	ayer	*ayyair*
tomorrow	mañana	*man-yah-na*
the day before yesterday	anteayer	*anteh-ayyair*
the day after tomorrow	pasado mañana	*passah-doh man-yah-na*
this week	esta semana	*esta semah-na*
next week	la semana que viene	*la semah-na keh vyeh-neh*
this morning	esta mañana	*esta man-yah-na*
this afternoon	esta tarde	*esta tardeh*
this evening	esta tarde/noche	*esta tardeh/notcheh*
tonight	esta noche	*esta notcheh*
yesterday afternoon	ayer por la tarde	*ayyair por la tardeh*
last night	anoche	*annotcheh*
tomorrow morning	mañana por la mañana	*man-yah-na por la man-yah-na*
tomorrow night	mañana por la noche	*man-yah-na por la notcheh*
in three days	dentro de tres días	*dentroh deh tress dee-ass*
three days ago	hace tres días	*ah-theh tress dee-ass*
late	tarde	*tardeh*
early	temprano	*temprah-noh*
soon	pronto	*prontoh*
later on	más tarde	*mass tardeh*
at the moment	en este momento	*en esteh momentoh*
second	un segundo	*segoondoh*
minute	un minuto	*meenootoh*
quarter of an hour	un cuarto de hora	*kwartoh deh ora*
half an hour	media hora	*meh-dya ora*
three quarters of an hour	tres cuartos de hora	*tress kwartoss deh ora*

hour	la hora	_ora_
day	el día	_dee_-a
every day	todos los días	_todoss loss dee_-ass
all day	todo el día	_todoh el dee_-a
the next day	al día siguiente	al _dee_-a seeg_yenteh
week	la semana	sem_ah_-na
month	el mes	mess
year	el año	_ahn_-yoh

Telling Time

The 24-hour clock is used in Spain, both in the written form (as in timetables) and verbally (e.g. in inquiry offices). However, you will still hear the 12-hour clock used in everyday life.

"O'clock" is not normally translated in Spanish unless it is for emphasis, when **en punto** would be used. For example: **(es) la una (en punto)** is "(it's) one o'clock." The plural form of the verb is used for all other hours, e.g. **(son) las cinco (en punto)** is "(it's) five o'clock."

The word "past" is translated as **y** (= "and"). In order to express minutes after the hour, state the hour followed by **y** plus the number of minutes: so **las seis y diez** is "ten past six." The word "to" is translated as **menos** (= "less"). So, for example, **las diez menos veinte** is "twenty to ten." The word for "quarter" is **cuarto**; **las siete menos cuarto** is "quarter to seven" and **las cinco y cuarto** is "quarter past five." The half hour is expressed using **y media**, so **las seis y media** is "6:30."

The word "at" is translated as **a** followed by **las**. For example, **a las tres y cuarto** is "at quarter past three." Remember to change **las** to **la** when using "one," thus "at 1:30" becomes **a la una y media**.

The expressions "AM" and "PM" have no direct equivalents, but the expressions **de la mañana** (in the morning), **de la tarde** (in the afternoon/evening—which extends up to 8 PM in Spain), and **de la noche** (at night—i.e. from 8 PM) are used to distinguish between times that might otherwise be confusing.

For example, "6 AM" is **las seis de la mañana** and "6 PM" is **las seis de la tarde**; "10 AM" is **las diez de la mañana** and "10 PM" is **las diez de la noche**.

what time is it?	¿qué hora es?	*keh ora ess*
AM	de la mañana	*deh la man-yah-na*
PM *(up to 8 PM)*	de la tarde	*deh la tardeh*
(from 8 PM)	de la noche	*deh la notcheh*
one o'clock	la una	*la oona*
ten past one	la una y diez	*la oona ee dyeth*
quarter past one	la una y cuarto	*la oona ee kwartoh*
1:30	la una y media	*la oona ee meh-dya*
twenty to two	las dos menos veinte	*lass doss meh-noss vaynteh*
quarter to two	las dos menos cuarto	*lass doss meh-noss kwartoh*
two o'clock	las dos (en punto)	*lass doss (en poontoh)*
13:00	las trece horas	*lass treh-theh orass*
16:30	las dieciséis treinta	*lass dyeth-ee-sayss traynta*
20:10	las veinte diez	*lass vaynteh dyeth*
at seven o'clock	a las siete	*a lass see-eh-teh*
noon	mediodía	*meh-dyoh dee-a*
midnight	medianoche	*meh-dya notcheh*

THE CALENDAR

The cardinal numbers on page 19 are used to express the date in Spanish. However, sometimes in formal Spanish, the ordinal number may be used instead, but only to express "the first":

May first	el uno/el primero de mayo	*el oonoh/el preemeh-roh deh mayyoh*
June twentieth	el veinte de junio	*el vaynteh deh Hoon-yoh*

22

HOTELS

Hotels are divided into five classes (with star ratings), followed by the **pensiones** (guesthouses), which have three. Farther down the scale come the **hotel residencia** for longer stays and the **hostal**, which is similar to a **pensión**. **Casas Rurales** are country houses whose owners accept visitors. The previously state-run **paradores** are superior (often converted castles, palaces, etc.) and allow unlimited stays, although you will have to pay for the extra comfort and scenery. If traveling in peak season, it is always advisable to reserve accommodations in advance in the more popular areas.

USEFUL WORDS AND PHRASES

balcony	el balcón	bal-kon
bath (*tub*)	la bañera	ban-yeh-ra
bathroom	el cuarto de baño	kwartoh deh bahn-yoh
bed	la cama	kah-ma
bed and breakfast	alojamiento y desayuno	aloh-ʜamyentoh ee dessa-yoonoh
bedroom	la habitación	abbee-tath-yon
bill	la cuenta	kwenta
breakfast	el desayuno	dessa-yoonoh
dining room	el comedor	kommeh-dor
dinner	la cena	theh-na
double bed	la cama doble, la cama de matrimonio	kah-ma doh-bleh, kah-ma deh matreemonyoh
double room	una habitación doble	abbee-tath-yon doh-bleh
elevator	el ascensor	ass-then-sor
foyer	el hall	ʜol
full board	pensión completa	penss-yon kompleh-ta
guesthouse	la pensión	penss-yon
half board	media pensión	meh-dya penss-yon
hotel	el hotel	oh-tell
key	la llave	yah-veh
lounge	el salón	sa-lon

lunch	la comida	*komee-da*
maid	la camarera	*kamareh-ra*
manager	el director	*deerek-tor*
parking lot	el aparcamiento	*aparkamyentoh*
receipt	la factura	*fak-toora*
reception	la recepción	*reh-thepth-yon*
receptionist	el recepcionista	*reh-thepth-yoneesta*
restroom	los servicios	*vattair, retreh-teh*
room	la habitación	*abbee-tath-yon*
room service	el servicio de	*sairveeth-yoh deh*
	habitaciones	*abbeetath-yoh-ness*
shower	la ducha	*dootcha*
single bed	la cama individual	*kah-ma eendeeveed-wal*
single room	una habitación	*abbee-tath-yon*
	individual	*eendeeveed-wal*
sink	el lavabo	*lavah-boh*
twin room	una habitación	*abbee-tath-yon kon*
	con dos camas	*doss kah-mass*

Do you have any vacancies?
¿Tienen alguna habitación libre?
tyeh-nen algoona abbee-tath-yon leebreh

I have a reservation
He hecho una reserva
eh etchoh oona reh-sairva

I'd like a single room
Quería una habitación individual
keh-ree-a oona abbee-tath-yon eendeeveed-wal

I'd like a room with a balcony/bathroom
Quería una habitación con balcón/cuarto de baño
keh-ree-a oona abbee-tath-yon kon bal-kon/kwartoh deh bahn-yoh

Is there satellite/cable TV in the rooms?
¿Hay televisión por satélite/por cable en las habitaciones?
i televeesseeon por sateleete/por kable en las abblee-tath-yoh-ness

I'd like a room for one night/three nights
Quería una habitación para una noche/para tres noches
keh-ree-a oona abbee-tath-yon parra oona notcheh/parra tress notcess

What is the charge per night?
¿Cuál es la tarifa por noche?
kwal ess la tarreefa por notcheh

I don't yet know how long I'll stay
Todavía no sé cuánto tiempo me voy a quedar
todavee-a noh seh kwantoh tyempoh meh voy a keh-dar

When is breakfast/dinner?
¿A qué hora es el desayuno/la cena?
a keh ora ess el dessa-yoonoh/la theh-na

Please wake me at … o'clock
Haga el favor de llamarme a las …
ah-ga el fa-vor deh yamar-meh a lass

May I have breakfast in my room?
¿Pueden servirme el desayuno en mi habitación?
pweh-den sair-veermeh el dessa-yoonoh en mee abbee-tath-yon

I'd like to have some laundry done
Quisiera utilizar el servicio de lavado
keess-yeh-ra ooteeleethar el sairveeth-yoh deh lavah-doh

I'll be back at … o'clock
Volveré a las …
volveh-reh a lass

My room number is …
El número de mi habitación es el …
el noomeh-roh deh mee abbee-tath-yon ess el

My reservation was for a double room
Había reservado una habitación doble
abee-a resairvah-doh oona abbee-tath-yon doh-bleh

I asked for a room with private bathroom
Pedí una habitación con baño
peh-dee oona abbee-tath-yon kon bahn-yoh

The lamp is broken
La lámpara está rota
la lampara esta rohta

There is no toilet paper in the bathroom
No hay papel higiénico en el cuarto de baño
noh ı papel ee-Hyeneekoh en el kwartoh deh bahn-yoh

The window won't open
No se puede abrir la ventana
noh seh pweh-deh abreer la ventah-na

There isn't any hot water
No hay agua caliente
noh ı ahg-wa kalyenteh

The outlet in the bathroom doesn't work
El enchufe del cuarto de baño no funciona
el entchoofeh del kwartoh deh bahn-yoh noh foonthyoh-na

I'm leaving tomorrow
Me marcho mañana
meh martchoh man-yah-na

When do I have to vacate the room?
¿A qué hora tengo que desocupar la habitación?
a keh ora teng-goh keh dessokoopar la abbee-tath-yon

Can I have the bill, please?
¿Me da la cuenta, por favor?
meh da la kwenta por fa-vor

I'll pay by credit card
Pagaré con tarjeta (de crédito)
pagareh kon tar-Heh-ta deh kredeetoh

I'll pay cash
Pagaré al contado
*pagar**eh** al kont**ah**doh*

Can you get me a taxi?
¿Puede llamar a un taxi?
*pw**eh**-deh yam**ar** a oon t**a**ksee*

Can you recommend another hotel?
¿Puede recomendarme otro hotel?
*pw**eh**-deh rekomend**ar**meh **o**troh oh-t**e**ll*

THINGS YOU'LL SEE

acceso prohibido	staff only
albergue	country hotel
almuerzo	lunch
alojamiento y desayuno	bed and breakfast
aparcamiento	parking, parking lot
ascensor	elevator
baño	bath
cena	dinner
CH	boardinghouse
comedor	dining room
comida	lunch, meal
completo	no vacancies
cuarto de baño	bathroom
cuenta	bill
desayuno	breakfast
empujar	push
entrada	entrance
escaleras	stairs
hotel-residencia	residential hotel
HR	residential hotel
media pensión	half board
parador	luxury hotel

→

27

pensión	guesthouse
pensión completa	full board
planta baja	ground floor
primer piso	second floor
prohibida la entrada	no admission
prohibido el paso	staff only
salida de emergencia	emergency exit
salón	lounge
servicio	restroom
solo para residentes	hotel patrons only
tirar	pull
WC	restroom

THINGS YOU'LL HEAR

Lo siento, está lleno
I'm sorry, we're full

El hotel está completo
We don't have any vacancies

No nos quedan habitaciones individuales/dobles
There are no single/double rooms left

¿Para cuántas noches?
For how many nights?

¿Va a pagar al contado, o con tarjeta?
Will you be paying by cash or credit card?

Haga el favor de pagar por adelantado
Please pay in advance

Tiene que desocupar la habitación antes de las doce
You must vacate the room by noon

CAMPING AND TRAILER TRAVEL

There are plenty of recognized sites all over Spain, especially along the Mediterranean coast, and most are open all year round. At other sites, you will need a permit from landowners or authorities such as the Forestry Authority. Ask the Spanish Tourist Office for details.

Youth hostels are open to members of the YHA, but in the peak season it is best to make a reservation in advance and stays are limited to three nights. You can get details from the Spanish Tourist Office in New York or local offices in Spain.

USEFUL WORDS AND PHRASES

backpack	la mochila	*motch__ee__la*
bucket	el cubo	*k__oo__-boh*
camper (RV)	la caravana	*karav__ah__-na*
camper site	un camping	*k__a__mpeen*
campfire	una hoguera	*oh-g__eh__-ra*
campsite	un camping	*k__a__mpeen*
go camping	ir de camping	*eer deh k__a__mpeen*
cooking utensils	los utensilios de cocina	*ootens__ee__l-yoss deh koth__ee__na*
drinking water	agua potable	*__ah__g-wa pott__ah__-bleh*
garbage	la basura	*bass__oo__ra*
groundcloth	la lona impermeable	*l__oh__-na eempair-meh-__ah__-bleh*
hitchhike	hacer auto-stop	*ath__ai__r owtoh-stop*
rope	una cuerda	*kw__ai__rda*
saucepans	las cazuelas	*kath-w__eh__-lass*
sleeping bag	el saco de dormir	*s__ah__-koh deh dorm__ee__r*
tent	la tienda	*ty__e__nda*
youth hostel	el albergue juvenil	*alb__ai__rgeh ʜooven__ee__l*

Can I camp here?
¿Puedo acampar aquí?
pw__eh__-doh akampar ak__ee__

29

Can we park the camper here?
¿Podemos aparcar aquí la caravana?
podeh-moss apar-kar akee la karavah-na

Where is the nearest campsite/camper site?
¿Dónde está el camping más cercano?
dondeh esta el kampeen mass thair-kah-noh

What is the charge per night?
¿Cuál es la tarifa por noche?
kwal ess la tarreefa por notcheh

How much is it for a week?
¿Cuánto es para una semana?
kwantoh ess parra oona sehmah-na

I only want to stay for one night
Es sólo para una noche
ess soh-loh parra oona notcheh

We're leaving tomorrow
Nos vamos mañana
noss vah-moss manyah-na

Where is the kitchen?
¿Dónde está la cocina?
dondeh esta la kotheena

Can I light a fire here?
¿Puedo encender fuego aquí?
pweh-doh enthen-dair fweh-goh akee

Where can I get ...?
¿Dónde puedo conseguir ...?
dondeh pweh-doh konseh-geer

Is there any drinking water?
¿Hay agua potable aquí?
ı ahg-wa pottah-bleh akee

THINGS YOU'LL SEE

agua	water
agua potable	drinking water
albergue juvenil	youth hostel
aseos	restroom
camping	campsite, camper site
cocina	kitchen
duchas	showers
fuego	fire
luz	light
manta	blanket
no se admiten perros	no dogs allowed
precio	price
prohibido …	no …
prohibido acampar	no camping
prohibido el paso	no trespassing
prohibido encender fuego	no campfires
saco de dormir	sleeping bag
se alquila	for rent
se prohíbe …	… forbidden
supermercado	supermarket
tarifa	charges
tienda	store
uso	use
WC	restroom

VILLAS AND APARTMENTS

You may be asked to pay for certain "extras" not included in the original price. You might want to ask if electricity, gas, etc., is included. It's a good idea to ask about an inventory of household goods at the beginning, rather than be told something is missing just as you are about to leave. You may be asked for a deposit, so make sure you get a receipt for it.

USEFUL WORDS AND PHRASES

agency	la agencia	*ah-Henthya*
bath (*tub*)	el baño	*bahn-yoh*
bathroom	el cuarto de baño	*kwartoh deh bahn-yoh*
bedroom	el dormitorio	*dormee-tor-yoh*
blind	la persiana	*perss-yahna*
blocked	atascado	*atass-kah-doh*
boiler	la caldera	*kaldeh-ra*
break	romper	*rompair*
broken	roto	*rohtoh*
caretaker	el encargado,	*enkargah-doh,*
	el portero	*porteh-roh*
central heating	la calefacción central	*kaleffakthyon thentral*
cleaner	la señora de la	*sen-yora deh la*
	limpieza	*leempyeh-tha*
comforter	el edredón	*edreh-don*
deposit	el depósito	*deh-posseetoh*
drain	el desagüe	*desahg-weh*
electrician	un electricista	*elektreetheesta*
electricity	la electricidad	*elektreetheedad*
faucet	un grifo	*greefoh*
fusebox	la caja de fusibles	*kah-Ha deh foosseebless*
gas	el gas	*gas*
garbage can	(el cubo de) la basura	*kooboh deh la bassoora*
grill	la parrilla, el grill	*parree-ya, greell*
heater	la estufa	*estoofa*
iron	la plancha	*plantcha*

ironing board	la tabla de planchar	*tah-bla deh plantchar*
key(s)	la(s) llave(s)	*la(ss) yahveh(ss)*
kitchen	la cocina	*kotheena*
leak (*in roof*)	una gotera	*gohteh-ra*
(*in pipe*)	un agujero	*ahgoo-Heh-roh*
light	la luz	*looth*
light bulb	la bombilla	*bombee-ya*
living room	el cuarto de estar	*kwartoh deh estar*
maid	la sirvienta	*seervyenta*
pillow	la almohada	*almoh-ahda*
pillowcase	la funda de almohada	*foonda deh almoh-ahda*
plumber	un fontanero,	*fontaneh-roh,*
	plomero	*plomeh-roh*
refrigerator	la nevera	*neh-veh-ra*
refund	un reembolso	*reh-embolsoh*
sheets	las sábanas	*sahbanass*
shower	la ducha	*dootcha*
sink	el fregadero	*fregadeh-roh*
stopper	la llave de paso	*yah-veh deh pah-soh*
stove	la cocina	*kotheena*
swimming pool	la piscina	*peessthee-na*
swimming pool	el encargado de la	*enkargah-doh deh la*
technician	piscina	*peessthee-na*
toilet	el retrete, el wáter	*retreh-teh, vattair*
towel	la toalla	*toh-ay-a*
washing machine	la lavadora	*lavadora*
water	el agua	*ahg-wa*
water heater	el calentador	*kalentador del ahg-wa*
	(del agua)	

Does the price include electricity/cleaning?
¿Está la electricidad/la limpieza incluída?
esta la elektreetheedad/la leempyeh-tha eenklweeda

Do I need to sign an inventory?
¿Hará falta que firme algún inventario?
ara falta keh feermeh algoon eembentaryoh

33

Where is this item?
¿Dónde está este artículo?
dondeh esta esteh arteekooloh

Please take it off the inventory
Haga el favor de quitarlo del inventario
ah-ga el fa-vor deh keetarloh del eembentaryoh

We've broken this
Se nos ha roto esto
seh noss a rohtoh estoh

This was broken when we arrived
Esto estaba roto cuando llegamos
estoh estah-ba rohtoh kwandoh yehgah-moss

This was missing when we arrived
Esto faltaba cuando llegamos
estoh faltah-ba kwandoh yehgah-moss

Can I have my deposit back?
¿Me devuelve el depósito?
meh deh-vwelveh el deh-posseetoh

Can we have an extra bed?
¿Puede ponernos otra cama más?
pweh-deh ponairnoss otra kah-ma mass

Can we have more dishes/cutlery?
¿Puede ponernos más platos y vasos/cubiertos?
pweh-deh ponairnoss mass plah-toss ee vah-soss/koob-yairtoss

Where is …?
¿Dónde está …?
dondeh esta

When does the maid come?
¿Cuándo viene la sirvienta?
kwandoh vyeh-neh la seervyenta

Where can I buy/find …?
¿Dónde podría comprar/encontrar …?
dondeh podree-a komprar/enkontrar

How does the water heater work?
¿Cómo funciona el calentador (de agua)?
koh-moh foonthyoh-na el kalentador deh ahg-wa

Do you do baby-sitting?
¿Hace usted de canguro?
ah-theh oosteh deh kan-goo-roh

Do you make lunch/dinner?
¿Prepara usted la comida/la cena?
prepah-ra oosteh la komee-da/la theh-na

Do we have to pay extra or is it included?
¿Hay que pagar aparte o está incluído en el precio?
I keh pagar aparteh oh esta eenklweedoh en el prethyoh

The shower doesn't work
No funciona la ducha
noh foonthyoh-na la dootcha

The sink is blocked
El fregadero está atascado
el fregadeh-roh esta ataskah-doh

The sink/toilet is leaking
Sale agua del fregadero/retrete
sah-leh ahg-wa del fregadeh-roh/retreh-teh

There's a burst pipe
Hay una cañería rota
I oona kan-yeree-a rohta

The roof leaks
Hay una gotera en el tejado
I oona gohteh-ra en el teh-Hah-doh

The tank leaks
Hay un agujero en el depósito
I oon ahgoo-Heh-roh en el deposseetoh

There's a gas leak
El gas se está saliendo
el gas seh esta salyendoh

The garbage has not been collected for three days
Llevan tres días sin recoger la basura
yeh-van tress dee-ass seen rekoh-Hair la bassoora

There's no electricity/gas/water
No hay luz/gas/agua
noh I looth/gas/ahg-wa

The bottled gas has run out—how do we get a new canister?
Se ha acabado el butano—¿cómo podemos conseguir otra
  bombona?
*seh ah akabah-doh el bootah-noh—koh-moh podeh-moss konsegeer
  oh-tra bomboh-na*

Can you fix it today?
¿Puede arreglarlo hoy?
pweh-deh arreglarlo oy

Send your bill to …
Mande la factura a …
mandeh la faktoora a

I'm staying at …
Estoy en …
estoy en

Thanks for looking after us so well
Gracias por tratarnos tan bien
grath-yass por tratarnoss tam byen

See you again next year
Hasta el año que viene
asta el ahn-yoh keh vyeh-neh

DRIVING

Spanish highways (**autopistas**) can be expensive to use because of the tolls. The best roads to use are the national main roads (**nacionales**). They often have passing lanes for heavy vehicles, especially on gradients. In recent years, however, many divided highways (**autovías**) have been built. However, secondary roads, **comarcales**, may be in quite poor condition.

The rule of the road is drive on the right, pass on the left. Secondary roads yield to major routes at intersections. In the case of roads having equal status, or at unmarked intersections, traffic coming from the **RIGHT** has priority. Look for the pictorial signs for priority on narrow bridges, etc. A system worth noting for changing direction or for crossing over divided highways is a semicircular exit ramp that is usually noted by **cambio de sentido**.

The speed limit on the **autovías** is 62 mph (100 km/h), and on the **autopistas** it's 75 mph (120 km/h). On **nacionales** it's 56 mph (90 km/h). In built-up areas the limit will vary between 25–35 mph (40—60 km/h).

Equipment to be carried at all times includes a spare set of light bulbs and a red triangle in case of breakdown or an accident. The traffic police patrols, **Guardia Civil de Tráfico**, will help you if you're in trouble, just as they will be ready to fine you on the spot should you break the law! Gas stations on the main roads are usually open 24 hours a day. They are seldom self-service. Unleaded gas is not readily available outside cities and main tourist areas. Fuel ratings are as follows: **extra** leaded, **gas-oil** diesel, **sin plomo** unleaded.

Parking in Spain is generally not restrictive—look for the signs, since there aren't any markings on the curb. In main towns and cities, however, the central area will come under what is often known as the **zona azul**, with only restricted parking allowed. Look for parking meters or the more common "pay and display" points. There are more and more underground parking lots, too, that operate on a ticket and barrier system.

SOME COMMON ROAD SIGNS

aduana	customs
apagar luces de cruce	headlights off
aparcamiento	parking lot
atención al tren	beware of trains
autopista	highway
autovía	divided highway
callejón sin salida	no thoroughfare
calle peatonal	pedestrians only
calzada deteriorada	bad surface
calzada irregular	uneven surface
cambio de sentido	intersection
carretera cortada	road closed
ceda el paso	yield
centro ciudad	city center
centro urbano	town center
circule despacio	slow
circunvalación	circular road
cruce	intersection
desvío	detour
desvío provisional	temporary detour
encender luces de cruce	headlights on
escalón lateral	no hard shoulder
escuela	school
final de autopista	end of highway
firme en mal estado	bad surface
hielo	black ice
información turística	tourist information
obras	road construction
ojo al tren	beware of trains
paso a nivel	train crossing
paso subterráneo	pedestrian underpass
peaje	toll
peatón, circule a la izquierda	pedestrians, keep to the left

peatones	pedestrians
peligro	danger
peligro deslizamientos	slippery road surface
precaución	caution
prohibido aparcar	no parking
prohibido el paso	no trespassing
puesto de socorro	first-aid station
salida de camiones	construction exit
vado permanente	in constant use (*no parking*)
vehículos pesados	heavy vehicles
velocidad controlada por radar	automatic speed monitor
zona azul	restricted parking zone
zona de estacionamento limitado	restricted parking area

USEFUL WORDS AND PHRASES

automatic	automático	*owtoh-mateekoh*
brake	el freno	*freh-noh*
breakdown	una avería	*avveh-ree-a*
car	el coche	*kotcheh*
clutch	el embrague	*embrah-geh*
divided highway	la autovía	*owtoh-vee-a*
drive	conducir	*kondoo-theer*
driver's license	el permiso/el carnet de conducir	*pairmeesso/karneh deh kondoo-theer*
engine	el motor	*moh-tor*
exhaust	el tubo de escape	*tooboh deh eskah-peh*
fanbelt	la correa del ventilador	*korreh-a del venteela-dor*
garage (*for repairs*)	un taller	*tayair*
gas	la gasolina	*gassoh-leena*
gas station	una gasolinera	*gassoh-leeneh-ra*
gear	la marcha	*martcha*
gears	las marchas	*mar-tchass*
headlights	las luces de cruce	*loothess deh kroo-theh*

highway	la autopista	*owtoh-peesta*
hood	el capó	*kapo*
intersection	el cruce	*kroo-theh*
junction	el cruce	*kroo-theh*
(highway entry)	un enlace de entrada	*enlah-theh deh entrah-da*
(highway exit)	un enlace de salida	*enlah-theh deh saleeda*
license plate	la matrícula	*matree-koola*
manual	manual	*man-wal*
mirror	el (espejo) retroviso	*esspeh-Hoh retroh-vessor*
motorcycle	la moto (cicleta)	*motoh-thee-kleh-ta*
parking lot	el aparcamiento	*aparkamyentoh*
road	la carretera	*karreh-teh-ra*
spare parts	los repuestos	*reh-pwestoss*
spark plug	la bujía	*boo-Hee-a*
speed	la velocidad	*velothee-da*
speed limit	el límite de velocidad	*leemeeth deh velothee-da*
speedometer	el cuentakilómetros	*kwenta-keelomeh-tross*
steering wheel	el volante	*voh-lanteh*
taillights	las luces traseras	*loothess-trasseh-rass*
tire	el neumático	*neh-oo-mateekoh*
tow	remolcar	*reh-molkar*
trailer	la caravana	*karra-vah-na*
transmission	la caja de velocidades	*kah-ha deh velotheedah-dess*
traffic lights	el semáforo	*seh-mafforoh*
trailer	el remolque	*reh-molkeh*
truck	el camión	*kam-yon*
trunk	el maletero	*malleh-teh-roh*
turn signal	intermitente	*eentairmeetenteh*
van	la furgoneta	*foorgoneh-ta*
wheel	la rueda	*rweh-da*
windshield	el parabrisas	*para-bree-sass*
windshield wiper	el limpiaparabrisas	*leempya-parabreessass*

I'd like some gas/oil/water
Quería gasolina/aceite/agua
keh-ree-a gassoh-leena/athay-teh/ahg-wa

Fill it up, please!
¡Lleno, por favor!
yeh-noh por fa-vor

35 liters of leaded gas, please
Póngame treinta y cinco litros de extra
ponga-meh traynti theenkoh leetross deh extra

Would you check the tires, please?
¿Podría revisar los neumáticos, por favor?
podree-a revee-sarmeh loss neh-oo-mateekoss por fa-vor

Do you do repairs?
¿Hacen reparaciones?
ah-then reparrath-yoh-ness

Can you repair the clutch?
¿Pueden arreglarme el embrague?
pweh-den arreh-glarmeh el embrah-geh

There is something wrong with the engine
Hay algo que no va bien en el motor
I algoh keh noh va byen en el moh-tor

The engine is overheating
El motor se calienta demasiado
el moh-tor seh kal-yenta deh-massyah-doh

I need a new tire
Necesito un neumático nuevo
neh-thessee-toh oon neh-oo-matikoh nweh-voh

Can you replace this?
¿Pueden cambiarme esto?
pwehden kambyarmeh estoh

The turn signal is not working
El intermitente no funciona
el eentairmeetenteh noh foonthyoh-na

How long will it take?
¿Cuánto tiempo tardarán?
kwantoh tyempoh tardaran

I'd like to rent a car
Quería alquilar un coche
keh-ree-a alkee-lar oon kotcheh

I'd like an automatic/a manual
Quiero un coche automático/manual
kyeroh oon kotcheh owtoh-mateekoh/man-wal

How much is it for one day?
¿Cuánto cuesta para un día?
kwantoh kwesta parra oon dee-a

Is there a mileage charge?
¿Tiene suplemento por kilómetro?
tyeh-neh sooplementoh por keelometroh

When do I have to return it?
¿Cuándo tengo que devolverlo?
kwandoh teng-goh keh devolvairloh

Where is the nearest garage?
¿Dónde está el taller más cercano?
dondeh esta el tayair mass thair-kah-noh

Where is the nearest gas station?
¿Dónde está la gasolinera más cercana?
dondeh esta la gassoh-leeneh-ra mass thair-kah-na

Where can I park?
¿Dónde puedo aparcar?
dondeh pweh-doh appar-kar

Can I park here?
¿Puedo aparcar aquí?
pw<u>eh</u>-doh appar-k<u>a</u>r ak<u>ee</u>

How do I get to Seville?
¿Cómo se va a Sevilla?
k<u>oh</u>-moh seh va a sev<u>ee</u>-ya

Is this the road to Malaga?
¿Es ésta la carretera de Málaga?
ess <u>e</u>sta la karreh-t<u>eh</u>-ra deh m<u>a</u>laga

Which is the quickest way to Madrid?
¿Cuál es el camino más rápido para Madrid?
kwal ess el kam<u>ee</u>noh mass r<u>a</u>peedoh p<u>a</u>rra madr<u>ee</u>d

---

DIRECTIONS YOU MAY BE GIVEN

a la derecha/izquierda	on the right/left
después de pasar el/la …	go past the …
la primera a la derecha	first on the right
la segunda a la izquierda	second on the left
todo recto	straight ahead
tuerza a la derecha	turn right
tuerza a la izquierda	turn left

THINGS YOU'LL SEE

aceite	oil
agua	water
aire	air
apague el motor	turn off engine
aparcamiento subterráneo	underground parking lot
área de servicios	service area, highway services
cola	line (of cars)

→

completo	parking lot full
entrada	entrance
estación de servicio	service station
extra	leaded
garaje	garage
gas-oil	diesel
gasolina	gas, fuel
gasolinera	gas station
introduzca el dinero exacto	exact change
nivel del aceite	oil level
presión	air pressure
presión de los neumáticos	tire pressure
prohibido fumar	no smoking
recoja su ticket	take a ticket
reparación	repairs
salida	exit
sin plomo	unleaded
solo para residentes del hotel	hotel guests only
taller (de reparaciones)	garage (for repairs)
(tren de) lavado automático	car wash

THINGS YOU'LL HEAR

¿Lo quiere automático o manual?
Would you like an automatic or a manual?

Su permiso/carnet de conducir, por favor
May I see your driver's license?

Su pasaporte, por favor
Your passport, please

TRAVELING AROUND

Air Travel

Numerous international airlines provide services to Spanish destinations including Madrid, Barcelona, Bilbao, Valencia, Alicante, Malaga, Seville, Santiago, Tenerife, and Las Palmas in the Canaries, and Palma, Menorca, and Ibiza in the Balearic Islands. There is also a domestic network connecting the main cities in Spain.

Train Travel

The Spanish national railroad system is called **RENFE** (*ren-fay*). Most trains are slow when compared to long-distance buses, even between major cities, but they are reasonably comfortable and inexpensive. The main types of trains are:

AVE	High-speed train covering the Madrid–Seville line.
TALGO and TER	Fast diesel trains with air conditioning; you pay a supplement in addition to the normal fare. The **TALGO** is much more luxurious than the **TER**.
TAF	Slower diesel train used on secondary routes.
Exprés	A misleading name, since this is a slow night train stopping at all stations.
Rápido	Also misleading since it is just a daytime version of the **Exprés**.
Automotor Cercanías Ferrobús Omnibús	Local short-distance trains.

Long-Distance Bus Travel

There is an excellent bus network covering all of Spain, giving a better connecting service between cities than, and covering the gaps in, the railroad system. The buses are comfortable and fast, and have facilities such as video and air conditioning.

LOCAL BUSES

All Spanish cities have a good bus system. Most buses are one-person operated and you pay the driver as you enter. Since there is generally a flat fare, it is less expensive to buy a book of tickets called a **bonobús**. There are also other types of tickets.

SUBWAY

Madrid, Barcelona, Valencia, and Bilbao have a subway system, the **metro**. You can pick up information about tickets and prices at stations and tourist information centers.

BOAT AND TAXI

There is a daily boat service to the Balearics (usually overnight) and a less frequent service to the Canaries, taking about two days. There is also a daily ferry linking Algeciras to North African ports such as Tangiers, Ceuta, and Melilla.

Taxis display a green light at night, and a sign on the windshield says if they are available (**libre**).

USEFUL WORDS AND PHRASES

adult	un adulto	ad_oo_l-toh
airport	el aeropuerto	ah-airoh-pw_ai_r-toh
airport bus	el autobús del aeropuerto	owtoh-b_oo_ss del ah-airoh-pw_ai_r-toh
aisle seat	un asiento de pasillo	ass-y_e_ntoh deh pass_ee_-yoh
baggage claim	la recogida de equipajes	rekoh-H_ee_da deh ekee-p_ah_-hess
boarding pass	la tarjeta de embarque	tar-H_eh_-ta deh emb_a_r-keh
boat	el barco billetes	b_a_rkoh bee-y_eh_-tess
buffet	la cafetería	kaffeh-teh-r_ee_-a
bus	el autobús	owtoh-b_oo_ss
bus station	la estación de autobuses	estath-y_o_n deh owtoh-b_oo_ssess
bus stop	la parada del autobús	par_ah_-da del owtoh-b_oo_ss

car (train)	el vagón	va-gon
check in desk	el mostrador de facturación	mostra-dor deh faktoorath-yon
child	un niño/una niña	neen-yoh/neen-yah
compartment	el compartimento	kompartee-mentoh
connection	un enlace	enlah-theh
cruise	un crucero	krootheh-roh
currency exchange	el cambio de moneda	kamb-yoh deh monneh-da
customs	aduana	ad-wah-na
departure lounge	salidas	salee-dass
dining car	el vagón-restaurante	va-gon restow-ranteh
dock	el muelle	mweh-yeh
domestic	nacional	nath-yonal
driver	el conductor	kondook-tor
emergency exit	la salida de emergencia	salee-da deh eh-mair-Henth-ya
entrance	la entrada	entrah-da
exit	la salida	salee-da
fare	el billete	bee-yeh-teh
ferry	el ferry	ferree
first class	primera (clase)	preemeh-ra klah-seh
flight	el vuelo	vweh-loh
flight number	el número de vuelo	noomeh-roh deh vweh-loh
gate	la puerta (de embarque)	pwair-ta deh embar-keh
international	internacional	eentairnath-yonal
lost and found	la oficina de objetos perdidos	offee-theena deh ob-Heh-toss pairdee-doss
luggage cart	un carrito para el equipaje	karree-toh parra el ekee-pah-Heh
luggage storage office	la consigna	konseeg-na
nonsmoking	no fumadores	noh fooma-doress
number 5 bus	el (autobús número) cinco	owtoh-booss noomeh-roh theenkoh

one-way ticket	un billete de ida	*bee-yeh-teh deh eeda*
passport	el pasaporte	*passa-porteh*
platform	el andén	*an-den*
port	el puerto	*pwair-toh*
railroad	el ferrocarril	*ferroh-karreel*
reservation office	el despacho de	*dess-patchoh deh*
reserved seat	un asiento reservado	*ass-yentoh reh-sair-vah-doh*
round-trip ticket	un billete de ida y vuelta	*bee-yeh-teh deh eeda ee vwel-ta*
seat	un asiento	*ass-yentoh*
second class	segunda (clase)	*segoonda klah-seh*
sleeper car	el coche-cama	*kotcheh kah-ma*
station	la estación	*estath-yon*
subway	el metro	*meh-troh*
taxi	un taxi	*taksee*
terminal (*bus*)	la terminal	*tairmee-nal*
(*subway*)	la estación terminal	*estath-yon tairmee-nal*
ticket	un billete	*bee-yeh-teh*
timetable	el horario	*oh-rar-yoh*
train	el tren	*tren*
transit system map	un plano	*plah-noh*
underground passage	paso subterráneo	*passoh soob-terrah-neh-oh*
waiting room	la sala de espera	*sah-la deh espeh-ra*
window seat	un asiento de ventanilla	*ass-yentoh deh ventanee-ya*

AIR TRAVEL

A nonsmoking seat, please
Un asiento en la sección de no fumadores, por favor
oon ass-yentoh en la sekth-yon deh noh fooma-doress por fa-vor

I'd like a window seat, please
Quería un asiento junto a la ventanilla, por favor
keh-ree-a oon ass-yentoh Hoontoh a la ventanee-ya por fa-vor

How long will the flight be delayed?
¿Cuánto retraso lleva el vuelo?
kwantoh reh-trah-soh yeh-va el vweh-loh

Which gate for the flight to …?
¿Cuál es la puerta de embarque para el vuelo de …?
kwal ess la pwair-ta deh embar-keh parra el vweh-loh deh

TRAIN, BUS, AND SUBWAY TRAVEL

When does the train/bus for Cadiz leave?
¿A qué hora sale el tren/autobús para Cádiz?
a keh ora sah-leh el tren/owtoh-booss parra kah-deeth

When does the train/bus from Barcelona arrive?
¿A qué hora llega el tren/autobús de Barcelona?
a keh ora yeh-ga el tren/owtoh-booss deh bartheh-loh-na

When is the next train/bus to Alicante?
¿A qué hora sale el próximo tren/autobús para Alicante?
a keh ora sah-leh el prok-seemoh tren/owtoh-booss parra aleekanteh

When is the first/last train/bus to Saragossa?
¿A qué hora sale el primer/último tren/autobús para Zaragoza?
a keh ora sah-leh el preemair/ool-teemoh tren/owtoh-booss parra tharagoh-tha

What is the fare to Granada?
¿Cuánto cuesta el billete para Granada?
kwantoh kwesta el bee-yeh-teh parra granahda

Do I have to pay a supplement?
¿Tengo que pagar suplemento?
teng-goh keh pagar soopleh-mentoh

Do I have to change?
¿Tengo que hacer transbordo?
teng-goh keh athair tranz-bordoh

Does the train/bus stop at Salamanca?
¿Para el tren/autobús en Salamanca?
pah-ra el tren/owtoh-booss en salamanka

How long does it take to get to Cordoba?
¿Cuánto tiempo se tarda en llegar a Córdoba?
kwantoh tyempoh seh tar-da en yeh-gar a kordohba

Where can I buy a ticket?
¿Dónde puedo sacar un billete?
dondeh pweh-doh sakar oon bee-yeh-teh

A one-way/round-trip ticket to Gerona, please
Un billete de ida/de ida y vuelta a Gerona, por favor
oon bee-yeh-teh deh eeda/deh eeda ee vwel-ta a Herrohna por fa-vor

Is there a discount for children?
¿Hay precios especiales para niños?
i pretheeos espethyales parra neen-yoss

Could you help me get a ticket?
¿Podría usted ayudarme a sacar un billete?
podree-a oosteh ayoo-darmeh a sakar oon bee-yeh-teh

REPLIES YOU MAY BE GIVEN

El próximo tren sale a las dieciocho horas
The next train leaves at 18:00

Haga transbordo en Salamanca
Change at Salamanca

Tiene que pagar suplemento
You must pay a supplement

Ya no quedan asientos para Madrid
There are no more seats available for Madrid

I'd like to reserve a seat
Quería reservar un asiento
keh-ree-a reh-sair-var oon ass-yentoh

Is this the right train/bus for Almeria?
¿Es éste el tren/autobús para Almería?
ess esteh el tren/owtoh-booss parra almeh-ree-a

Is this the right platform for the Seville train?
¿Es éste el andén para el tren de Sevilla?
ess esteh el an-den parra el tren deh sev-ee-ya

Which platform for the Granada train?
¿Cuál es el andén para el tren de Granada?
kwahl ess el an-den parra el tren deh granahda

Is the train/bus late?
¿Lleva retraso el tren/autobús?
yeh-va reh-trah-soh el tren/owtoh-booss

Could you help me with my luggage, please?
¿Puede ayudarme con estas maletas, por favor?
pweh-deh ayoodar-meh kon estass maleh-tas por fa-vor

Is this a nonsmoking car?
¿Está prohibido fumar aquí?
esta pro-ee-beedoh foomar akee

Is this seat free?
¿Está libre este asiento?
esta leebreh esteh ass-yentoh

This seat is taken
Este asiento está ocupado
esteh ass-yentoh esta okoopah-doh

I have reserved this seat
Tengo reservado este asiento
teng-goh reh-sair-vah-doh esteh ass-yentoh

TRAVELING AROUND

May I open/close the window?
¿Puedo abrir/cerrar la ventana?
pweh-doh abreer/therrar la ventah-na

When do we arrive in Bilbao?
¿A qué hora llegamos a Bilbao?
a keh ora yeh-gah-moss a beelbah-oh

What station is this?
¿Qué estación es ésta?
keh estath-yon ess esta

Do we stop at Aranjuez?
¿Paramos en Aranjuez?
parah-moss en aran-Hweth

Is there a dining car on this train?
¿Lleva vagón-restaurante este tren?
yeh-va va-gon restow-ranteh esteh tren

Where is the nearest subway station?
¿Dónde está la estación de metro más cercana?
dondeh esta la estath-yon deh meh-troh mass thair-kah-na

Where is there a bus stop?
¿Dónde hay una parada de autobús?
dondeh I oona parah-da deh owtoh-booss

Which buses go to Merida?
¿Qué autobuses van a Mérida?
keh owtoh-boossess van a meh-reeda

How often do the buses to Madrid run?
¿Cada cuánto tiempo pasan los autobuses para Madrid?
kah-da kwantoh tyempoh pah-san loss owtoh-boossess parra madree

Will you let me know when we're there?
¿Puede avisarme cuando lleguemos?
pweh-deh aveess-armeh kwandoh yeh-geh-moss

Do I have to get off yet?
¿Tengo que bajarme ya?
teng-goh keh ba-Harmeh ya

How do you get to Nerja?
¿Cómo se va a Nerja?
koh-moh seh va a nair-Ha

Do you go near San Pedro?
¿Pasa usted cerca de San Pedro?
pah-sa oosteh thair-ka deh san peh-droh

TAXI AND BOAT

Where can I get a taxi?
¿Dónde puedo tomar un taxi?
dondeh pweh-doh tomar oon taksee

I want to go to …
Quiero ir a …
kee-eh-roh eer a

Can you let me off here?
Pare aquí, por favor
pah-reh akee por fa-vor

How much is it to El Escorial?
¿Cuánto cuesta ir a El Escorial?
kwantoh kwesta eer a el eskoree-al

Could you wait here for me and take me back?
¿Puede esperarme aquí y llevarme de vuelta?
pweh-deh espeh-rar-meh akee ee yeh-var-meh deh vwelta

Where can I get a ferry to Palma?
¿Dónde se puede coger un ferry para Palma?
dondeh seh pweh-deh koh-Hair oon ferree parra palma

THINGS YOU'LL SEE

abstenerse de fumar	no smoking, please
aduana	customs
adultos	adults
a los andenes	to the trains
andén	platform
asientos	seats
automotor	local short-distance train
AVE	high-speed train
billete/billetes	ticket/tickets, ticket office
billete de andén	platform ticket
bocadillos	sandwiches, snacks
bonobús	book of 10 bus tickets
cambio de moneda	currency exchange
coche-cama	sleeping car
consigna	luggage storage office
control de pasaportes	passport control
demora	delay
días azules	cheap travel days
domingos y festivos	Sundays and national holidays
entrada	entrance
entrada por delante/por detrás	entry at the front/rear
equipaje	luggage
escala	intermediate stop
estación principal	central station
excepto domingos	Sundays excepted
exprés	slow night train
facturación	check-in
ferrobús	local short-distance train
fumadores	smokers
hacer transbordo en ...	change at ...
hora local	local time
horario	timetable
laborables	weekdays

→

libre	vacant
llegadas	arrivals
multa por uso indebido	penalty for misuse
nacional	domestic
niños	children
no fumadores	nonsmokers
no para en ...	does not stop in ...
ocupado	occupied
pague el importe exacto	no change given
parada	stop
prensa	newsstand
prohibida la entrada	no entry
prohibido asomarse a la ventana	do not lean out of the window
prohibido el paso	no entry
prohibido fumar	no smoking
prohibido hablar con el conductor	do not speak to the driver
puerto	harbor
puerta de embarque	gate
puesto de periódicos	newsstand
rápido	slow train stopping at all stations
recogida de equipajes	baggage claim
RENFE	Spanish national railroads
reserva de asientos	seat reservation
retraso	delay
ruta	route
sala de espera	waiting room
salida	departure; exit
salida de emergencia	emergency exit
salidas	departures
sólo laborables	weekdays only
suplemento	supplement
TAF	slow diesel train
TALGO	fast diesel train

→

taquilla	ticket office
tarjeta	travel card
TER	fast diesel train
terminal	terminal
trenes de cercanías	local trains
utilice solo moneda fraccionaria	small change only
vagón	passenger car
viaje	trip
vuelo	flight
vuelo directo	direct flight
vuelo regular	scheduled flight

THINGS YOU'LL HEAR

¿Tiene equipaje?
Do you have any luggage?

¿Fumadores o no fumadores?
Smoking or nonsmoking?

¿Asiento de ventanilla o de pasillo?
Window seat or aisle seat?

Su billete, por favor
Can I see your ticket, please?

Los pasajeros del vuelo dos dos uno, con destino a Chicago, están en estos momentos embarcando
Passengers for flight 221 for Chicago are requested to board

Diríjanse a la puerta (número) cuatro
Please go to gate (number) four now

→

Completo
It's full

Los billetes, por favor
Tickets, please

Suban al tren
Board the train

El tren con destino a Granada va a efectuar su salida del andén número seis dentro de diez minutos
The train for Granada will leave from platform six in ten minutes

El tren procedente de Madrid va a efectuar su llegada al andén número uno dentro de cinco minutos
The train from Madrid will arrive at platform one in five minutes

El tren con destino a Sevilla lleva quince minutos de retraso
The train for Seville is running 15 minutes late

Saquen sus billetes, por favor
Have your tickets ready, please

Su pasaporte, por favor
Your passport, please

Abra sus maletas, por favor
Open your suitcases, please

EATING OUT

You can eat in a variety of places:

Restaurante: These have an official rating (1–5 forks), but this depends more on the variety of dishes served than on the quality.

Cafetería: Not to be confused with the American term. It is a combined bar, café, and restaurant. Service is provided at the counter or, for a little extra, at a table. There is usually a good variety of fixed-price menus at reasonable prices (look for **platos combinados**).

Fonda: Offers inexpensive, good food that is representative of regional dishes.

Hostería or Hostal: A restaurant that usually specializes in regional dishes.

Parador: Belonging to the previously state-run hotels, they offer a first-rate service in select surroundings.

Café or Bar: Both are general cafés selling all kinds of food and drink (again, they are not to be confused with American establishments of the same name). Well worth trying if you just want a quick snack. In some places, they serve free **tapas** (appetizers) with alcoholic drinks. Full meals are often available.

Merendero: Outdoor **café** on the coast or in the country. Usually inexpensive and a good buy.

Breakfast in Spain is at 8 AM, lunch is at 2 PM, and dinner (the main evening meal) is at 10 PM.

USEFUL WORDS AND PHRASES

appetizer	el primer plato	*primair plah-toh*
beer	una cerveza	*thairveh-tha*
bottle	la botella	*boh-tay-ya*

bread	el pan	*pan*
butter	la mantequilla	*manteh-kee-ya*
café	una cafetería	*kaffeh-teh-ree-a*
cake	un pastel	*pastell*
carafe	una jarra	*Harra*
check	la cuenta	*kwenta*
chef	el cocinero	*kothee-neh-roh*
children's	una ración especial	*rath-yon espethyal*
portion	para niños	*parra neen-yoss*
coffee	el café	*kaffeh*
cup	la taza	*tah-tha*
dessert	el postre	*postreh*
fork	el tenedor	*teneh-dor*
glass	el vaso	*vah-soh*
half liter	medio litro	*meh-dyoh leetroh*
knife	el cuchillo	*kootchee-yoh*
liter	litro	*leetroh*
main course	el segundo plato	*segoondoh plah-toh*
menu	la carta	*karta*
milk	la leche	*letcheh*
napkin	la servilleta	*sairvee-yeh-ta*
pepper	la pimienta	*peemyenta*
plate	el plato	*plah-toh*
receipt	un recibo	*retheeboh*
restaurant	un restaurante	*restowranteh*
salt	la sal	*sal*
sandwich	un sandwich	*sand-weetch*
(Spanish)	un bocadillo	*boh-kadee-yoh*
soup	la sopa	*soh-pa*
spoon	la cuchara	*kootchah-ra*
sugar	el azúcar	*athookar*
table	una mesa	*meh-sa*
tea	el té	*teh*
teaspoon	la cucharilla	*kootcha-ree-ya*
tip	una propina	*propeena*
waiter	el camarero	*kamma-reh-roh*

waitress	la camarera	*kamma-reh-ra*
water	el agua	*ahg-wa*
wine	el vino	*veenoh*
wine list	la carta de vinos	*karta deh veenoss*

A table for one, please
Una mesa para una persona, por favor
oona meh-sa parra oona pairsoh-na por fa-vor

A table for two/three, please
Una mesa para dos/tres personas, por favor
oona meh-sa parra doss/tress pairsoh-nass por fa-vor

Is there a highchair?
¿Hay sillita de niño?
i see-yeeta deh neen-yo

Can we see the menu/wine list?
¿Nos trae la carta/la carta de vinos?
noss trah-eh la karta/la karta deh veenoss

What would you recommend?
¿Qué recomendaría usted?
keh rekomenda-ree-a oosteh

I'd like …
Quería …
keh-ree-a

Just a cup of coffee, please
Un café nada más, por favor
oon kaffeh nah-da mass por fa-vor

I only want a snack
Sólo quiero una comida ligera
soh-loh kee-eh-roh oona kommeeda lee-Heh-ra

Is there a fixed-price menu?
¿Hay menú del día?
i meh-noo dell dee-a

A liter carafe of house red, please
Una jarra de litro de tinto de la casa, por favor
oona Harra deh leetroh deh teentoh deh la kah-sa por fa-vor

Do you have any vegetarian dishes?
¿Tiene algún plato vegetariano?
tyeh-neh algoon plah-toh veh-Hetaryah-noh

I'm allergic to nuts/shellfish
Soy alérgico a los frutos secos/marisco
soy allairheekoh a los frootos sekos/mareesko

Could we have some water?
¿Nos trae agua, por favor?
noss trah-eh ahg-wa por fa-vor

Two more beers, please
Dos cervezas más, por favor
doss thair-veh-thass mass por fa-vor

Do you have children's portions?
¿Tiene raciones especiales para niños?
tyeh-neh rathyoh-ness espethyah-less parra neen-yoss

Can you warm this bottle/baby food for me?
¿Podría calentar este biberón/comida para niño?
po-dreea kalentar este beeberon/komeeda parra neen-yoh

Waiter/waitress!
¡Oiga, por favor!
oy-gah por fa-vor

I didn't order this
No he pedido esto
noh eh pedeedoh estoh

You've forgotten to bring my dessert
Se ha olvidado de traerme el postre
seh a olveedah-doh deh trah-airmeh el postreh

May we have some more …?
¿Nos trae más …?
noss tr<u>ah</u>-eh mass

Can I have another knife/fork?
¿Me trae otro cuchillo/tenedor?
meh tr<u>ah</u>-eh <u>o</u>troh kootch<u>ee</u>-yoh/teneh-d<u>o</u>r

May we have the check, please?
¿Nos trae la cuenta, por favor?
noss tr<u>ah</u>-eh la kw<u>e</u>nta por fa-v<u>o</u>r

Could I have a receipt, please?
¿Me puede dar un recibo, por favor?
meh pweh-d<u>e</u>h dar oon reth<u>ee</u>boh por fa-v<u>o</u>r

Can we pay separately?
Queríamos pagar por separado
keh-r<u>ee</u>-amoss pag<u>a</u>r por separ<u>ah</u>-doh

The meal was very good, thank you
La comida ha sido muy buena, gracias
la komm<u>ee</u>da a s<u>ee</u>doh mwee bw<u>e</u>h-na gr<u>ah</u>th-yass

---

THINGS YOU'LL HEAR

¡Que (le/les) aproveche!
Enjoy your meal!

¿Qué quiere beber/tomar?
What would you like to drink?

¿Le ha gustado la comida?
Did you enjoy your meal?

62

MENU GUIDE

aceitunas	olives
acelgas	spinach beet
achicoria	chicory
aguacate	avocado
ahumados	smoked fish
ajo	garlic
albaricoques	apricots
albóndigas	meatballs
alcachofas	artichokes
alcachofas con jamón	artichokes with ham
alcachofas salteadas	sautéed artichokes
alcachofas a la vinagreta	artichokes vinaigrette
alcaparras	capers
almejas	clams
almejas a la marinera	clams stewed in wine and parsley
almejas naturales	live clams
almendras	almonds
alubias con ...	beans with ...
ancas de rana	frogs' legs
anchoas	anchovies
anguila	eel
angulas	baby eels
anís	aniseed-flavored alcoholic drink
arenque	herring
arroz a la cubana	rice with fried eggs and banana fritters
arroz a la valenciana	rice with seafood
arroz con leche	rice pudding
asados	roast meats
atún	tuna
avellanas	hazelnuts
azúcar	sugar
bacalao a la vizcaína	cod served with ham, peppers, and chilis
bacalao al pil pil	cod served with chilis and garlic
batido de chocolate	chocolate milk shake
batido de fresa	strawberry milk shake
batido de frutas	fruit milk shake
batido de vainilla	vanilla milk shake
bebidas	drinks

berenjenas	eggplant
besugo al horno	baked sea bream
bistec de ternera	veal steak
bizcochos	ladyfingers
bonito al horno	baked tunafish
bonito con tomate	tuna with tomato
boquerones fritos	fried anchovies
brazo gitano	swiss roll
brevas	figs
brocheta de riñones	kidney kebabs
buñuelos	light fried pastries
butifarra	Catalan sausage (made with a large proportion of bacon)
cabrito asado	roast goat
cachelada	pork stew with eggs, tomato, and onion
café	coffee
café con leche	coffee with steamed milk
calabacines	zucchini, vegetable marrow
calabaza	pumpkin
calamares a la romana	squid rings in batter
calamares en su tinta	squid cooked in their ink
calamares fritos	fried squid
caldeirada	fish soup
caldereta gallega	vegetable stew
caldo de ...	... soup
caldo de gallina	chicken soup
caldo de pescado	clear fish soup
caldo gallego	vegetable soup
caldo guanche	soup made with potatoes, onions, tomatoes, and zucchini
callos a la madrileña	tripe cooked with chilis
camarones	baby prawns
canelones	canneloni
cangrejos de río	river crabs
caracoles	snails
caramelos	candies
carnes	meats
carro de queso	cheese board
castañas	chestnuts
cebolla	onion
cebolletas	spring onions

centollo	spider crab
cerezas	cherries
cerveza	beer
cesta de frutas	a selection of fresh fruit
champiñón a la crema	mushrooms in cream sauce
champiñón al ajillo	mushrooms with garlic
champiñón a la plancha	grilled mushrooms
champiñón salteado	sautéed mushrooms
chanquetes	fish (similar to whitebait)
chateaubrian	Chateaubriand steak (thick steak)
chipirones	baby squid
chipirones en su tinta	squid cooked in their ink
chipirones rellenos	stuffed squid
chirimoyas	custard apples
chocos	squid
chuleta de buey	beef chop
chuleta de cerdo	pork chop
chuleta de cerdo empanada	breaded pork chop
chuleta de cordero	lamb chop
chuleta de ternera	veal chop
chuleta de ternera empanada	breaded veal chop
chuletas de cordero empanadas	breaded lamb chops
chuletas de lomo ahumado	smoked pork chops
chuletitas de cordero	small lamb chops
chuletón	large chop
chuletón de buey	large beef chop
churros	deep-fried pastry strips
cigalas	crayfish
cigalas cocidas	boiled crayfish
ciruelas	plums, greengages
ciruelas pasas	prunes
cochinillo asado	roast suckling pig
cocido	stew made with meat, chickpeas, and vegetables
cocktail de bogavante	lobster cocktail
cocochas (de merluza)	hake stew
cóctel de gambas	shrimp cocktail
cóctel de langostinos	jumbo shrimp cocktail
cóctel de mariscos	seafood cocktail
codornices	quail
codornices asadas	roast quail

codornices con uvas	quail stewed with grapes
codornices escabechadas	marinated quail
codornices estofadas	braised quail
col	cabbage
coles de Bruselas	Brussels sprouts
coles de Bruselas salteadas	sautéed Brussels sprouts
coliflor	cauliflower
coliflor con bechamel	cauliflower with white sauce
coñac	brandy
conejo asado	roast rabbit
conejo encebollado	rabbit served with onions
conejo estofado	braised rabbit
congrio	conger eel
consomé al jerez	consommé with sherry
consomé con yema	consommé with egg yolk
consomé de ave	fowl consommé
consomé de pollo	chicken consommé
contra de ternera con guisantes	veal stew with peas
contrafilete de ternera	veal fillet
copa …	… cup, glass of wine
copa de helado	ice cream, assorted flavors
cordero asado	roast lamb
cordero chilindrón	lamb stew with onion, tomato, peppers, and eggs
costillas de cerdo	pork ribs
crema catalana	crème brûlée
cremada	dessert made with egg, sugar, and milk
crema de cangrejos	cream of crab soup
crema de espárragos	cream of asparagus soup
crema de legumbres	cream of vegetable soup
crepe imperiale	crêpe suzette
criadillas de tierra	truffles, usually served with meat dishes
crocante	ice cream with chopped nuts
croquetas	croquettes
croquetas de jamón	ham croquettes
croquetas de pescado	fish croquettes
cuajada	curds
dátiles	dates
embutidos	sausages
embutidos de la tierra	local sausages
embutidos variados	assorted sausages

empanada gallega	fish pie
empanada santiaguesa	fish pie
empanadillas de bonito	small tuna pies
empanadillas de carne	small meat pies
empanadillas de chorizo	Spanish sausage pies
endivias	endive
ensaimada mallorquina	large, spiral-shaped bun
ensalada de arenque	fish salad
ensalada de atún	tuna salad
ensalada de frutas	fruit salad
ensalada de gambas	shrimp salad
ensalada de lechuga	lettuce salad
ensalada de pollo	chicken salad
ensalada de tomate	tomato salad
ensalada ilustrada	mixed salad
ensalada mixta	mixed salad
ensalada simple	green salad
ensalada	Spanish salad
ensaladilla rusa	Russian salad (potatoes, carrots, peas, and other vegetables in mayonnaise)
entrecot a la parrilla	grilled entrecôte
entrecot de ternera	veal entrecôte
entremeses de la casa	hors d'oeuvres, appetizers
entremeses variados	hors d'oeuvres, appetizers
escalope a la milanesa	breaded veal with cheese
escalope a la parrilla	grilled veal
escalope a la plancha	grilled veal
escalope de lomo de cerdo	escalope of pork fillet
escalope de ternera	veal scallop
escalope empanado	breaded scallops
escalopines al vino de Marsala	veal scallops cooked in wine
escalopines de ternera	veal scallops
escarola	escarole
espadín a la toledana	kabob
espaguetis italiana	spaghetti
espárragos	asparagus
espárragos con mayonesa	asparagus with mayonnaise
espárragos trigueros	green asparagus
espinacas	spinach
espinacas a la crema	creamed spinach
espinazo de cerdo con patatas	stew of pork ribs with potatoes

estofado de ...	... stew
estofado de liebre	hare stew
estofados	stews
estragón	tarragon
fabada (asturiana)	bean stew with sausage
faisán con castañas	pheasant with chestnuts
faisán estofado	stewed pheasant
faisán trufado	pheasant with truffles
fiambres	cold meats
fideos	thin pasta, noodles
filete a la parrilla	grilled beef
filete de cerdo	pork steak
filete de ternera	veal steak
flan	crème caramel
flan al ron	crème caramel with rum
flan de caramelo	crème caramel
fresas con nata	strawberries and cream
fruta	fruit
frutas en almíbar	fruit in syrup
fruta variada	assorted fresh fruit
gallina en pepitoria	chicken stewed with peppers
gambas al ajillo	garlic shrimp
gambas a la americana	shrimp
gambas a la plancha	grilled shrimp
gambas cocidas	boiled shrimp
gambas con mayonesa	shrimp with mayonnaise
gambas en gabardina	shrimp in batter
gambas rebozadas	shrimp in batter
garbanzos	chickpeas
garbanzos a la catalana	chickpeas with sausage, boiled eggs, and pine nuts
gazpacho andaluz	cold tomato soup from Andalusia
gelatina de ...	... gelatin
gratén de ...	... au gratin (baked in a cream and cheese sauce)
grelo	turnip
guisantes con jamón	peas with ham
guisantes salteados	sautéed peas
habas	broad beans
habas con jamón	broad beans with ham
habas fritas	fried young broad beans

habichuelas	beans
helado de caramelo	caramel ice cream
helado de chocolate	chocolate ice cream
helado de fresa	strawberry ice cream
helado de mantecado	vanilla ice cream
helado de turrón	nut ice cream
helado de vainilla	vanilla ice cream
hígado	liver
hígado con cebolla	liver cooked with onion
hígado de ternera estofado	braised calf's liver
hígado estofado	braised liver
higos con miel y nueces	figs with honey and nuts
higos secos	dried figs
horchata (de chufas)	cold almond-flavored milk drink
huevo hilado	egg yolk garnish
huevos	eggs
huevos a la flamenca	fried eggs with ham, tomato, and vegetables
huevos cocidos	hard-boiled eggs
huevos con jamón	eggs with ham
huevos duros	hard-boiled eggs
huevos duros con mayonesa	boiled eggs with mayonnaise
huevos con panceta	eggs and bacon
huevos con patatas fritas	fried eggs and french fries
huevos con picadillo	eggs with minced sausage
huevos con salchichas	eggs and sausages
huevos escalfados	poached eggs
huevos fritos	fried eggs
huevos fritos con chorizo	fried eggs with Spanish sausage
huevos fritos con jamón	fried eggs with ham
huevos pasados por agua	soft-boiled eggs
huevos rellenos	stuffed eggs
huevos revueltos con tomate	scrambled eggs with tomato
jamón con huevo hilado	ham with egg yolk garnish
jamón de Jabugo	Spanish ham
jamón de Trevélez	Spanish ham
jamón serrano	cured ham
jarra de vino	wine jug
jerez amontillado	pale dry sherry
jerez fino	pale light sherry
jerez oloroso	sweet sherry
jeta	pigs' cheeks

judías verdes	green beans
judías verdes a la española	bean stew
judías verdes al natural	plain green beans
judías verdes con jamón	green beans with ham
jugo de albaricoque	apricot juice
jugo de lima	lime juice
jugo de limón	lemon juice
jugo de melocotón	peach juice
jugo de naranja	orange juice
jugo de piña	pineapple juice
jugo de tomate	tomato juice
Jumilla	light red and white "mistela" wines
langosta a la americana	lobster with brandy and garlic
langosta a la catalana	lobster with mushrooms and ham in a white sauce
langosta fría con mayonesa	cold lobster with mayonnaise
langosta gratinada	lobster au gratin
langostinos a la plancha	grilled jumbo shrimp
langostinos con mayonesa	jumbo shrimp with mayonnaise
langostinos dos salsas	jumbo shrimp cooked in two sauces
laurel	bay leaves
leche frita	pudding made from milk and eggs
leche merengada	cold milk with meringues
lechuga	lettuce
lengua de buey	ox tongue
lengua de cordero estofada	stewed lambs' tongue
lenguado a la parrilla	grilled sole
lenguado a la plancha	grilled sole
lenguado a la romana	sole in batter
lenguado frito	fried sole
lenguado grillado	grilled sole
lenguado meuniere	sole meunière (sole dipped in flour, fried, and served with butter, lemon juice, and parsley)
lentejas	lentils
lentejas aliñadas	lentils in vinaigrette dressing
licores	spirits, liqueurs
liebre estofada	stewed hare
lombarda rellena	stuffed red cabbage
lombarda salteada	sautéed red cabbage
lomo curado	pork loin sausage

lonchas de jamón	sliced, cured ham
longaniza	cooked Spanish sausage
lubina a la marinera	sea bass in a parsley sauce
lubina al horno	baked sea bass
macarrones	macaroni
macarrones gratinados	macaroni and cheese
macedonia de fruta	fruit salad
Málaga	sweet wine
mandarinas	tangerines
manises	peanuts
manitas de cordero	lamb shank
manos de cerdo	pigs' feet
manos de cerdo a la parrilla	grilled pigs' feet
mantecadas	small sponge cakes
mantequilla	butter
manzanas	apples
manzanas asadas	baked apples
manzanilla	dry sherry-type wine
mariscada	cold mixed shellfish
mariscos del día	fresh shellfish
mariscos del tiempo	seasonal shellfish
mazapán	marzipan
medallones de anguila	eel steaks
medallones de merluza	hake steaks
media de agua	half bottle of mineral water
mejillones	mussels
mejillones a la marinera	mussels in a wine sauce
melocotón	peach
melocotones en almíbar	peaches in syrup
melón	melon
melón con jamón	melon with ham
membrillo	quince jelly
menestra de legumbres	vegetable stew
menú de la casa	fixed-price menu
menú del día	fixed-price menu
merluza a la cazuela	stewed hake
merluza a la parrilla	grilled hake
merluza a la plancha	grilled hake
merluza a la riojana	hake with chilis
merluza a la romana	hake steaks in batter
merluza a la vasca	hake in a garlic sauce

merluza al ajo arriero	hake with garlic and chillis
merluza en salsa	hake in sauce
merluza en salsa verde	hake in a parsley and wine sauce
merluza fría	cold hake
merluza frita	fried hake
mermelada	jam
mermelada de albaricoque	apricot jam
mermelada de ciruelas	prune jam
mermelada de frambuesas	raspberry jam
mermelada de fresas	strawberry jam
mermelada de limón	lemon marmalade
mermelada de melocotón	peach jam
mermelada de naranja	orange marmalade
mero	grouper (type of fish)
mero a la parrilla	grilled grouper
mero en salsa verde	grouper in garlic and parsley sauce
mollejas de ternera fritas	fried sweetbreads
morcilla	blood sausage
morcilla de carnero	blood sausage made from mutton
morros de cerdo	pigs' cheeks
morros de vaca	cows' cheeks
mortadela	salami-type sausage
morteruelo	kind of pâté
mousse de chocolate	chocolate mousse
mousse de limón	lemon mousse
nabo	turnip
naranjas	oranges
natillas	cold custard
natillas de chocolate	cold custard with chocolate
níscalos	wild mushrooms
nísperos	medlars (fruit similar to crab apple)
nueces	walnuts
orejas de cerdo	pigs' ears
otros mariscos según precios en plaza	other shellfish, depending on current prices
paella	fried rice with various seafood and chicken
paella castellana	meat paella
paella de marisco	shellfish paella
paella de pollo	chicken paella
paella valenciana	shellfish, rabbit, and chicken paella
paleta de cordero lechal	shoulder of lamb

pan	bread
pan de higos	dried fig cake with cinnamon
panache de verduras	vegetable stew
panceta	bacon
parrillada de caza	mixed grilled game
parrillada de mariscos	mixed grilled shellfish
pasas	raisins
pastel de ...	... cake
pastel de ternera	veal pie
pasteles	cakes
patatas a la pescadora	potatoes with fish
patatas asadas	baked potatoes
patatas bravas	potatoes in cayenne pepper sauce
patatas fritas	french fries
patitos rellenos	stuffed duckling
pato a la naranja	duck à l'orange
pato asado	roast duck
pato estofado	stewed duck
pavo asado	roast turkey
pavo relleno	stuffed turkey
pavo trufado	turkey stuffed with truffles
pecho de ternera	breast of veal
pechuga de pollo	breast of chicken
pepinillos	pickles
pepinillos en vinagreta	pickles in vinaigrette sauce
pepino	cucumber
peras	pears
percebes	edible barnacle (shellfish)
perdices a la campesina	partridges with vegetables
perdices a la manchega	partridges in red wine with garlic, herbs, and pepper
perdices asadas	roast partridges
perdices con chocolate	partridges with chocolate sauce
perdices escabechadas	marinated partridges
perejil	parsley
pescaditos fritos	fried fish
pestiños	sugared pastries flavored with aniseed
pez espada ahumado	smoked swordfish
picadillo de ternera	minced veal
pimienta	black pepper
pimientos a la riojana	baked red peppers fried in oil and garlic

pimientos fritos	fried peppers
pimientos morrones	bell peppers
pimientos rellenos	stuffed peppers
pimientos verdes	green peppers
piña al gratín	pineapple au gratin
piña fresca	fresh pineapple
pinchitos	snacks served in bars
pinchos	snacks served in bars
pinchos morunos	kebabs
piñones	pine nuts
pisto	fried mixed vegetables
pisto manchego	vegetable marrow with onion and tomato
plátanos	bananas
plátanos flameados	flambéed bananas
pollo a la parrilla	grilled chicken
pollo a la riojana	chicken with peppers and chilis
pollo al ajillo	fried chicken with garlic
pollo al champaña	chicken in champagne
pollo al vino blanco	chicken in white wine
pollo asado	roast chicken
pollo braseado	braised chicken
pollo con tomate	chicken with tomatoes
pollo con verduras	chicken and vegetables
pollo en cacerola	chicken casserole
pollo en pepitoria	chicken in wine with saffron, garlic, and almonds
pollo salteado	sautéed chicken
pollos tomateros con zanahorias	young chicken with carrots
polvorones	sugar-based dessert eaten at Christmas
pomelo	grapefruit
potaje castellano	thick broth
potaje de garbanzos	chickpea stew
potaje de habichuelas	white bean stew
potaje de lentejas	lentil stew
puchero canario	casserole of meat, chickpeas, and corn
pulpitos con cebolla	baby octopus with onions
pulpo	octopus
puré de patatas	mashed potatoes, potato purée
purrusalda	cod with leeks and potatoes
queso con membrillo	cheese with quince jelly
queso de Burgos	soft white cheese

queso de bola	Dutch cheese
queso de oveja	sheep's cheese
queso del país	local cheese
queso gallego	creamy cheese
queso manchego	hard, strong cheese
quisquillas	shrimps
rábanos	radish
ragout de ternera	veal ragoût
rape a la americana	monkfish with brandy and herbs
rape a la cazuela	stewed monkfish
rape a la plancha	grilled monkfish
raviolis	ravioli
raya	skate
redondo al horno	roast fillet of beef
remolacha	beets
repollo	cabbage
repostería de la casa	cakes baked on the premises
requesón	cream cheese, cottage cheese
revuelto de ajos tiernos	scrambled eggs with spring garlic
revuelto de angulas	scrambled eggs with baby eels
revuelto de gambas	scrambled eggs with shrimps
revuelto de sesos	scrambled eggs with brains
revuelto de trigueros	scrambled eggs with asparagus
revuelto mixto	scrambled eggs with mixed vegetables
Ribeiro	type of white wine
riñones	kidneys
riñones al jerez	kidneys with sherry
Rioja	red or white wine—considered the finest wine in Spain
rodaballo	turbot (*fish*)
romero	rosemary
ron	rum
roscas	sweet pastries
sal	salt
salchichas	sausages
salchichas de Frankfurt	hot dogs
salchichón	white sausage with pepper
salmón a la parrilla	grilled salmon
salmón ahumado	smoked salmon
salmón frío	cold salmon
salmonetes	red mullet

salmonetes a la parrilla	grilled red mullet
salmonetes en papillote	red mullet cooked in foil
salmorejo	thick sauce made with bread, tomatoes, olive oil, vinegar, green pepper, and garlic, usually served with hard-boiled eggs
salpicón de mariscos	shellfish vinaigrette
salsa allioli or ali oli	mayonnaise with garlic
salsa bechamel	white sauce
salsa de tomate	tomato sauce
salsa holandesa	hollandaise sauce (hot sauce made with eggs and butter)
salsa mahonesa or mayonesa	mayonnaise
salsa tártara	tartare sauce
salsa vinagreta	vinaigrette sauce
sandía	watermelon
sangría	sangría (mixture of red wine, lemonade, liquor, and fruit)
sardinas a la brasa	barbecued sardines
sardinas a la parrilla	grilled sardines
sardinas fritas	fried sardines
seco	dry
semidulce	medium-sweet
sesos a la romana	fried brains in batter
sesos rebozados	brains in batter
setas a la plancha	grilled mushrooms
setas rellenas	stuffed mushrooms
sidra	cider
sobreasada	soft red sausage with cayenne pepper
solomillo con guisantes	fillet steak with peas
solomillo con patatas	fillet steak with french fries
solomillo de ternera	fillet of veal
solomillo de vaca	fillet of beef
solomillo frío	cold roast beef
sopa	soup
sopa castellana	vegetable soup
sopa de ajo	garlic soup
sopa de almendras	almond-based pudding
sopa de cola de buey	oxtail soup
sopa de fideos	noodle soup
sopa de gallina	chicken soup

sopa del día	soup of the day
sopa de legumbres	vegetable soup
sopa de lentejas	lentil soup
sopa de marisco	fish and shellfish soup
sopa de pescado	fish soup
sopa de rabo de buey	oxtail soup
sopa de verduras	vegetable soup
sopa mallorquina	soup with tomato, meat, and eggs
sopa sevillana	fish and mayonnaise soup
sorbete	sorbet
soufflé	soufflé
soufflé de fresones	strawberry soufflé
soufflé de naranja	orange soufflé
soufflé de queso	cheese soufflé
suplemento de verduras	extra vegetables
tallarines	noodles
tallarines a la italiana	tagliatelle
tarta de almendra	almond cake
tarta de chocolate	chocolate cake
tarta de fresas	strawberry tart or cake
tarta de la casa	cake baked on the premises
tarta de manzana	apple tart
tarta helada	ice cream cake
tarta moca	mocha tart
tencas	tench
ternera asada	roast veal
tocinillos del cielo	crème caramel
tomates rellenos	stuffed tomatoes
tomillo	thyme
tordo	thrush
torrijas	sweet pastries
tortilla Alaska	baked Alaska
tortilla a la paisana	omelette with a variety of vegetables
tortilla a su gusto	omelette made to the customer's wishes
tortilla de bonito	tuna omelette
tortilla de champiñones	mushroom omelette
tortilla de chorizo	omelette containing spiced sausage
tortilla de escabeche	fish omelette
tortilla de espárragos	asparagus omelette
tortilla de gambas	shrimp omelette
tortilla de jamón	ham omelette

MENU GUIDE

tortilla de patatas	potato omelette
tortilla de sesos	brain omelette
tortilla de setas	mushroom omelette
tortilla española	Spanish omelette with potato, onion, and garlic
tortilla sacromonte	vegetable, brains, and sausage omelette
tortillas variadas	assorted omelettes
tournedó	tournedos (fillet steak)
trucha ahumada	smoked trout
trucha con jamón	trout with ham
trucha escabechada	marinated trout
truchas a la marinera	trout in wine sauce
truchas molinera	trout meunière (trout dipped in flour, fried, and served with butter, lemon juice, and parsley)
trufas	truffles
turrón	nougat
turrón de Alicante	hard nougat
turrón de Jijona	soft nougat
turrón de coco	coconut nougat
turrón de yema	nougat with egg yolk
uvas	grapes
Valdepeñas	type of fruity red wine
vieiras	scallops
vino blanco	white wine
vino de mesa	table wine
vino rosado	rosé wine
vino tinto	red wine
zanahorias a la crema	carrots à la crème
zarzuela de mariscos	seafood stew
zarzuela de pescados y mariscos	fish and shellfish stew
zumo de ...	... juice
zumo de albaricoque	apricot juice
zumo de lima	lime juice
zumo de limón	lemon juice
zumo de melocotón	peach juice
zumo de naranja	orange juice
zumo de piña	pineapple juice
zumo de tomate	tomato juice

STORES AND SERVICES

This chapter covers all kinds of shopping needs and services.
To start with, you'll find some general phrases that can be used
in lots of different places—many of these are listed below.
After the general phrases come more specific requests and
sentences to use when you've found what you need, be it food,
clothing, repairs, film developing, a haircut, or bargaining in
the market. Don't forget to refer to the mini-dictionary for
items you may be looking for.

Stores can stay open as they wish, but most stick to the usual
hours of 9 AM to 1:30 PM and 4:30 PM to 7:30 PM. In summer, a
longer lunch break means that stores stay open in the evenings
from about 5 PM to 8:30 PM. Most stores close at 2 PM on
Saturdays. Large department stores do not close for lunch and
are open longer on Saturdays.

Toiletries and non-medicinal items can be bought from
supermarkets and department stores or from a **perfumería**,
where they'll probably cost a little more. (See Health, page 113,
for details about pharmacies.)

A hair salon is called a **peluquería**. A men's hair salon is often
called a **barbería**. It is easily recognized by the traditional
barber's pole or a similar device with red, white, and blue stripes.

USEFUL WORDS AND PHRASES

antiques store	la tienda de antigüedades	t_yenda deh antee-gwehd_ah-dess
audio equipment	aparatos de música	apar_ah-toss deh m_oossika
bakery	la panadería	pannadeh-r_ee-a
bookstore	la librería	leebreh-r_ee-a
butcher's	la carnicería	karnee-theh-r_ee-a
buy	comprar	kompr_ar
camera store	la tienda de fotografía	t_yenda deh fotografe_e-a
camping equipment	equipos de camping	ek_eeposs deh k_ampeen

carrier bag	una bolsa	_bolsa_
cash register	la caja	_kah_-нa
china	la porcelana	_porthelah-na_
confectioner's	la confitería	_konfeeteree-a_
cost	costar	_kostar_
craft shop	la tienda de artesanía	_tyenda deh artesanee-a_
department store	los grandes almacenes	_grandess almatheh-ness_
dry cleaner's	la tintorería	_teentoreree-a_
electrical goods store	la tienda de electrodomésticos	_tyenda deh elektro-domestee-koss_
expensive	caro	_kah-roh_
fish market	la pescadería	_peskadeh-ree-a_
florist's	la floristería	_floreess-teh-ree-a_
food store	la tienda de alimentación	_tyenda deh aleementath-yon_
gift shop	la tienda de regalos	_tyenda deh regah-loss_
hair salon (_men's_)	la barbería	_barbeh-ree-a_
(_women's_)	la peluquería	_pelookeh-ree-a_
hardware store	la ferretería	_ferreh-teh-ree-a_
indoor market	el mercado	_mairkah-doh_
inexpensive	barato	_barah-toh_
jeweler's	la joyería	_нoy-ehree-a_
large department store	el híper	_eepair_
Laundromat	la lavandería automática	_lavanderee-a owtoh-mateeka_
liquor store	la bodega de vinos	_boh-dehga deh veenos_
market	el mercadillo	_mairkadee-yoh_
menswear	caballeros	_kabayeh-ross_
newsstand	el kiosko de periódicos	_kee-oskoh deh peh-ree-oddee-koss_
optician's	la óptica	_opteeka_
pastry shop	la pastelería	_pasteh-leh-ree-a_
produce market	la frutería	_frooteree-a_

receipt	el recibo	*retheeboh*
record store	la tienda de discos	*tyenda deh deeskoss*
sale	rebajas, liquidación	*rebah-Hass, leekee-dath-yon*
shoe repairer's	reparación del calzado	*reparath-yon del kalthah-doh*
shoe store	la zapatería	*thapateh-ree-a*
souvenir store	la tienda de regalos	*tyenda deh regah-loss*
sports equipment	equipos de deporte	*eh-keeposs deh dehporteh*
sportswear	ropa de deporte	*roh-pa deh dehporteh*
stationery store	la papelería	*papeh-leh-ree-a*
store	la tienda	*tyenda*
supermarket	el supermercado	*sooper-mair-kah-doh*
tailor	la sastrería	*sastreh-ree-a*
tobacco shop	el estanco	*estankoh*
toy store	la juguetería	*Hoo-gheh-teh-ree-a*
travel agency	la agencia de viajes	*aHenth-ya deh vyah-Hess*
women's wear	señoras	*sen-yorass*

Excuse me, where is/are …? *(in a supermarket)*
Por favor, ¿dónde está/están …?
por fa-vor dondeh esta/estan

Where is there a … (store)?
¿Dónde hay una (tienda de) …?
dondeh I oona tyenda deh

Where is the … department?
¿Dónde está la sección de …?
dondeh esta la sekth-yon deh

Where is the main shopping area?
¿Dónde está la zona comercial?
dondeh esta la thona kommairth-yal

Is there a market here?
¿Hay algún mercado aquí?
I algoon mair-kah-doh akee

I'd like …
Quería …
keh-ree-a

Do you have …?
¿Tienen …?
tyeh-nen

How much is this?
¿Cuánto es esto?
kwantoh ess estoh

Where do I pay?
¿Dónde se paga?
dondeh seh pah-ga

Do you take credit cards?
¿Puedo pagar con tarjeta de crédito?
pweh-doh pagar kon tar-Heh-ta deh kredeetoh

I think perhaps you've shortchanged me
Me parece que me ha dado cambio de menos
meh pareh-theh keh meh a dadoh kamb-yoh deh menoss

Can I have a receipt?
¿Me da un recibo?
meh da oon retheeboh

Can I have a bag, please?
¿Me da una bolsa, por favor?
meh da oona bolsa por fa-vor

I'm just looking
Sólo estoy mirando
soh-loh estoy meerandoh

I'll come back later
Volveré luego
bolver__eh__ lw__eh__goh

Do you have any more of these?
¿Tiene alguno más de éstos?
ty__eh__-neh alg__oo__noh m__a__ss deh __e__stoss

Do you have anything less expensive?
¿Tiene usted algo más barato?
ty__eh__-neh oost__eh__ __a__lgoh mass bar__ah__-toh

Do you have anything larger/smaller?
¿Tiene usted algo más grande/pequeño?
ty__eh__-neh oost__eh__ __a__lgoh mass gr__a__ndeh/peh-k__ay__n-yoh

Can I try it (them) on?
¿Puedo probármelo(s)?
pw__eh__-doh prob__a__rmeh-loh(ss)

Does it come in other colors?
¿Lo hay en otros colores?
loh __i__ en __o__tross kol__o__ress

Could you gift wrap it for me?
¿Podría envolvérmelo para regalo?
podr__ee__-a embol-v__ai__rmeh-loh __p__arra reg__ah__-loh

I'd like to exchange this, it doesn't work
Quiero que me cambien esto porque tiene un defecto
ky__eh__-roh keh meh k__a__mbyen __e__stoh p__o__r-keh ty__eh__-neh oon def__e__ktoh

I'm afraid I don't have the receipt
Me temo que no tengo el recibo
meh t__e__moh keh noh t__e__ng-goh el res__ee__boh

Can I have a refund?
¿Pueden devolverme el dinero?
pw__eh__-den deh-volv__ai__r-meh el deen__eh__-roh

My camera isn't working
Mi cámara no funciona
mee kam-eh-ra noh foonth-yoh-na

I want a roll of 36-exposure color film. 100 ISO
Quiero un carrete en color de treinta y seis fotos. De cien ISO
kyeh-roh oon karreh-teh en kolor deh traynti sayss fotos deh thyen ee esseh oh

I'd like this film developed
Quería revelar este carrete
kehree-a revelar esteh karreh-teh

Matte prints
Copias en papel mate
koh-pyass en pappell mateh

Glossy prints
Copias con brillo
koh-pyass kon bree-yoh

One-hour service, please
Servicio de una hora, por favor
sairveeth-yoh deh oona ora por fa-vor

Where can I get this fixed?
¿Dónde me pueden arreglar esto?
dondeh meh pweh-den arreh-glar estoh

Can you fix this?
¿Puede arreglarme esto?
pweh-deh arrehglarmeh estoh

I'd like this skirt/these pants dry-cleaned
Quiero que me limpien esta falda/estos pantalones
kyeh-roh keh meh leempyen esta falda/estoss pantaloh-ness

When will it (they) be ready?
¿Cuándo estará(n) listo(s)?
kwandoh estara(n) leestoh(ss)

I'd like some change for the washing machine/dryer
¿Me puede cambiar dinero para la lavadora/secadora?
meh pweh-deh kambyar deeneh-roh parra la lavadora/sekadora

Can you help me work the machine, please?
¿Puede enseñarme a manejar la máquina, por favor?
pweh-deh ensen-yarmeh a maneh-Har la makeena por fa-vor

I'd like to make an appointment
Quería pedir hora
keh-ree-a pedeer ora

I want a cut and blow-dry
Quería un corte y moldeado con secador de mano
keh-ree-a oon korteh ee moldeh-ah-doh kon sekador deh mah-noh

With conditioner/No conditioner, thanks
Con acondicionador/Sin acondicionador, por favor
kon akondeeth-yonador/seen akondeeth-yonador por fa-vor

Just a trim, please
Recórtemelo un poco solamente, por favor
rekorteh-meh-loh oon pokoh sola-menteh por fa-vor

A bit more off here, please
Córtemelo un poco más por aquí, por favor
korteh-meh-loh oon pokoh mass por akee por fa-vor

Not too much off!
¡No me corte demasiado!
noh meh korteh demass-yah-doh

When does the market open?
¿Cuándo se abre el mercado?
kwandoh seh ah-breh el mair-kah-doh

What's the price per kilo?
¿Cuánto vale el kilo?
kwantoh valeh el keeloh

85

Could you write that down?
¿Puede escribírmelo?
pweh-deh eskreebeermeh-loh

That's too much! I'll pay …
¡Eso es demasiado! Le doy …
esso ess deh-mass-yah-doh! leh doy

I've seen that on another stall for … pesetas
Lo he visto en otro puesto a … pesetas
loh eh veestoh en otroh pwestoh a … peh-seh-tass

That's fine. I'll take it
Está bien. Me lo llevo
esta byen. meh loh yeh-voh

I'll have a piece of that cheese
Quiero un trozo de ese queso
kyeh-roh oon troh-thoh deh esseh keh-soh

About 250/500 grams
Como doscientos cincuenta/quinientos gramos
koh-moh dossthyentoss theen-kwenta/keenyentoss grah-moss

A kilo/half a kilo of apples, please
Un kilo/medio kilo de manzanas, por favor
oon keeloh/meh-dyoh keeloh deh manthah-nass por fa-vor

A quarter of a kilo of ham, please
Un cuarto de kilo de jamón, por favor
oon kwartoh deh keeloh deh Hamon por fa-vor

May I taste it?
¿Puedo probarlo?
pweh-doh probarloh

No, I don't like it
No, no me gusta
noh noh meh goosta

That's very nice. I'll take some
Está muy bueno. Me llevaré un poco
está mwee bw<u>eh</u>-noh. meh yehvar<u>eh</u> oon p<u>oh</u>-koh

It isn't what I wanted
No es lo que yo quería
noh ess loh keh yoh keh-r<u>ee</u>-a

THINGS YOU'LL SEE

abierto	open
agencia de viajes	travel agency
alimentación	groceries
alquiler	rental
autoservicio	self-service
barato	inexpensive
barbería	barber
bricolage	do-it-yourself supplies
caballeros	menswear
caja	cash register, checkout
calidad	quality
calzados	shoe store
carnicería	butcher's
cerrado	closed
cerrado por vacaciones	closed for holidays
cerramos los …	closed on …
droguería	household cleaning materials
estanco	tobacco shop
ferretería	hardware store
flores	flowers
ganga	bargain
grandes almacenes	department store
helados	ice cream parlor
juguetes	toys
lavado	shampoo, cleaning

→

librería	bookstore
liquidación total	stock clearance
moda	fashion
moldeado con secador de mano	blow-dry
no se admiten devoluciones	no refunds given
no tocar	do not touch
objetos de escritorio	office supplies
oferta	special offer
panadería	bakery
papelería	stationery store
pastelería	pastry shop
peletería	furrier
peluquería de caballeros	men's hairstylist
peluquería de señoras	women's salon
planta sótano	basement floor
planta superior	upper floor
por favor, use una cesta/un carrito	please take a basket/cart
precio	price
rebajado	reduced
rebajas	sales
rebajas de verano	summer sale
saldos	sales
salón de peluquería	hair salon
sección	department
señoras	women's department
verduras	vegetables

THINGS YOU'LL HEAR

¿Le están atendiendo?
Are you being served?

¿Qué desea?
Can I help you?

¿No tiene cambio?
Do you have anything smaller? (money)

Lo siento, se nos han terminado
I'm sorry, we're out of stock

Esto es todo lo que tenemos
This is all we have

No podemos devolver el importe
We cannot give cash refunds

¿Desea algo más?
Will there be anything else?

¿Cuánto quería?
How much would you like?

¿Le importa que sea un poco más?
Does it matter if it's a bit over?

Lo siento, no admitimos tarjetas de crédito
I'm afraid we don't take credit cards

¿Cómo quiere que se lo corte?
How would you like it cut?

SPORTS

Thanks to Spain's excellent climate, almost all outdoor sports are well represented. The east and south coasts especially provide excellent opportunities for swimming, water-skiing, sailing, fishing (including underwater fishing), and sailboarding. The north coast also has good facilities and is becoming more and more popular, despite the cooler climate. A flag warning system operates on most Atlantic beaches: red for dangerous conditions, yellow for caution, and green for all clear. Renting equipment is no problem, and everything from a beach umbrella to a sailboard is offered at a reasonable charge. Golf, which has become very popular, is played all year round, and there are courses in Madrid and nearly all the major beach resorts. Most golf courses offer lessons. Tennis courts can be found in most places and squash is gaining in popularity. Bicycling is very popular, and there are now more and more places where you can rent bicycles. In areas such as the Pyrenees and the Sierra Nevada, there is mountaineering, walking, and skiing in the winter.

USEFUL WORDS AND PHRASES

athletics	el atletismo	atleh-_teez_moh
badminton	el badminton	b_a_dmeen-ton
ball	la pelota	peh-l_oh_-ta
beginners' slope	la pista de principiantes	_pee_sta deh preentheepy_a_ntess
bicycle	una bicicleta	beethee-kl_eh_-ta
bicycle path	el carril para bicicletas	karr_ee_l parra beetheekl_eh_-tass
bicycling	el ciclismo	theekl_ee_zmoh
binding (ski)	una atadura	atad_oo_ra
bullfighting	los toros	t_oh_-ross
canoe	una piragua	peer_ah_-gwa
canoeing	el piragüismo	peerag-w_ee_zmoh
cross-country skiing	el esquí de fondo	esk_ee_ deh _f_ondoh

90

current	una corriente	*korryenteh*
dive	tirarse de cabeza	*teerarseh deh kabeh-tha*
diving board	un trampolín	*trampoh-leen*
fishing	la pesca	*peska*
fishing rod	una caña de pescar	*kahn-ya deh peskar*
flippers	las aletas	*aleh-tass*
game	un juego	*Hweh-goh*
goggles	las gafas de bucear	*gah-fass deh bootheh-ar*
golf	el golf	*golf*
play golf	jugar al golf	*Hoogar al golf*
golf club *(stick)*	el palo	*paloh*
golf course	un campo de golf	*kampoh deh golf*
gymnastics	la gimnasia	*Heemnass-ya*
hang gliding	el ala delta	*ala delta*
harpoon	el fusil submarino	*foo-seel soobma-reenoh*
go hiking	hacer senderismo	*athair sendaireezmoh*
hockey	el hockey	*Hokkay*
hunting	la caza	*katha*
mast	el mástil	*masteel*
mountaineering	el montañismo	*montan-yeezmoh*
oxygen bottles	las botellas de	*botay-yass deh*
	oxígeno	*oksee-Hennoh*
paragliding	el parapente	*parapenteh*
pedal boat	un hidropedal	*eedroh-peh-dal*
piste	la pista	*peesta*
Pyrenees	los Pirineos	*peereeneh-oss*
racket	una raqueta	*rakeh-ta*
ride	montar a caballo	*montar a kaba-yoh*
riding	la equitación	*ekeetath-yon*
riding hat	el casco de	*kaskoh deh*
	equitación	*ekeetath-yon*
rock climbing	el alpinismo	*alpeeneezmoh*
saddle	la silla	*see-ya*
sail *(noun)*	la vela	*veh-la*
(verb)	navegar (a vela)	*navegar a veh-la*
sailboard	una tabla de	*tah-bla deh*
	windsurfing	*weendsoorfeen*

sailing	vela	*veh-la*
go sailing	hacer vela	*athair veh-la*
skate (*verb*)	patinar	*pateenar*
skates	los patines	*patee-ness*
skating rink	la pista de patinaje	*peesta deh pateenah-Heh*
ski (*noun*)	un esquí	*eskee*
(*verb*)	esquiar	*eskyar*
ski boots	las botas de esquí	*botass deh eskee*
skiing	el esquí	*eskee*
ski lift	el telesquí	*tehlehskee*
skin diving	el submarinismo	*soobmaree-neezmoh*
ski pass	un abono	*aboh-noh*
ski poles	los bastones	*bastoh-ness*
ski tow	el remonte	*remonteh*
ski trail	la pista de fondo	*peesta deh fondoh*
ski wax	la cera de esquís	*theh-ra deh eskeess*
sled	el trineo	*treeneh-oh*
snorkel	el respirador	*resspeera-dor*
soccer ball	el balón	*ba-lon*
soccer match	un partido de fútbol	*partee-doh deh foot-bol*
sports center	el polideportivo	*poleedeporteevoh*
stadium	el estadio	*estah-dyoh*
surfboard	la tabla de surfing	*tabla deh soorfeen*
swim	nadar	*nadar*
swimming pool	la piscina	*peessthee-na*
team	el equipo	*ekeepoh*
tennis	el tenis	*teh-neess*
tennis court	una pista de tenis	*peesta deh teh-neess*
tennis racket	una raqueta de tenis	*rakeh-ta deh teh-neess*
toboggan	el tobogán	*tobogan*
underwater fishing	la pesca submarina	*peska soobmaree-na*
volleyball	el vóleibol	*vollay-bol*
water-skiing	el esquí acuático	*eskee akwatee-koh*
water skis	los esquís acuáticos	*eskeess akwatee-koss*

wet suit	un traje isotérmico	*trah-Heh eessoh-tairmee-koh*
go windsurfing	hacer windsurfing	*athair weendsoorfeen*
yacht	un yate	*yah-teh*

How do I get to the beach?
¿Por dónde se va a la playa?
por dondeh seh va a la pla-ya

How deep is the water here?
¿Qué profundidad tiene el agua aquí?
keh profoondee-da tyeh-neh el ah-gwa akee

Is there an indoor/outdoor pool here?
¿Hay piscina cubierta/al aire libre aquí?
I peessthee-na koob-yairta/al I-reh leebreh akee

Is it safe to swim here?
¿Se puede nadar sin peligro aquí?
seh pweh-deh nadar seen pelee-groh akee

Can I fish here?
¿Puedo pescar aquí?
pweh-doh peskar akee

Do I need a license?
¿Necesito un permiso?
nethessee-toh oon pair-meessoh

Is there a golf course near here?
¿Hay algún campo de golf por aquí cerca?
I algoon kampoh deh golf por akee thairka

Do I have to be a member?
¿Es necesario ser socio?
ess nethessaryoh sair soh-thyoh

I would like to rent a bicycle/some skis
Quería alquilar una bicicleta/unos esquís
keh-ree-a alkee-lar oona beethee-kleh-ta/oonoss eskeess

How much does it cost per hour/day?
¿Cuánto cuesta por hora/por día?
kwantoh kwesta por ora/por dee-a

I would like to take water-skiing lessons
Quería dar clases de esquí acuático
keh-ree-a dar klah-sess deh eskee akwatee-koh

Where can I rent …?
¿Dónde puedo alquilar …?
dondeh pweh-doh alkee-lar

There's something wrong with this binding
No sé qué pasa con esta atadura
noh seh keh pah-sa kon esta atadoora

How much is a weekly pass for the ski lift?
¿Cuánto valen los abonos semanales para el telesquí?
kwantoh balen loss aboh-noss semanah-less parra el tehlehskee

What are the snow conditions like today?
¿Cuál es el estado de la nieve hoy?
kwal ess el estadoh deh la nyeh-veh oy

I'd like to try cross-country skiing
Me gustaría probar el esquí de fondo
meh goostaree-a probar el eskee deh fondoh

I haven't played this before
Nunca había jugado a esto antes
noonka abee-a Hoogah-doh a estoh antess

Let's go skating/swimming
Vamos a patinar/nadar
bah-moss a pateenar/nadar

What's the score?
¿A cómo van?
a koh-moh van

Who won?
¿Quién ha ganado?
kyen a ganadoh

THINGS YOU'LL SEE

acceso playa	to the beach
alquiler de barcos	boat rental
alquiler de bicicletas	bike rental
alquiler de esquís	(water) ski rental
alquiler de sombrillas	umbrella rental
alquiler de tablas	board rental
alquiler de tumbonas	lounge chair rental
camino privado	private entrance
campo de golf	golf course
corriente peligrosa	dangerous current
palos de golf	golf clubs
peatones	pedestrians
peligro	danger
piscina	swimming pool
piscina cubierta	indoor swimming pool
pista de tenis	tennis court
prohibido bañarse	no swimming
prohibido el paso	no trespassing
prohibido encender fuego	no fires
prohibido pescar	no fishing
remonte	ski tow
socorrista	lifeguard
telecabina	cable car
telesilla	chair lift
telesquí	ski lift

POST OFFICES AND BANKS

Post offices in Spain deal only with mail, so don't look for a phone there. Use a phone booth or find the exchange (**Telefónica**). Stamps can be bought in the post office, but most Spaniards go to an **estanco** (a state tobacco shop—look for the brown and yellow sign) where you can also buy postcards. Mailboxes are yellow.

Banks are open half a day, usually from 9 AM to 1:30 PM Monday to Friday, although this may vary depending on where you are. They are also open on Saturdays until 1 PM. There are usually only one or two cashiers. First you have to go to the foreign exchange counter, **cambio**, and then line up for the cashier. However, more and more banks in large towns are changing over to the system where all transactions take place at the same counter. ATMs are widespread.

The Spanish unit of currency is the **peseta**. Coins come in denominations of 5, 10, 25, 50, 100, 200, and 500 **pesetas**. Bills are available in 1,000, 2,000, 5,000, and 10,000 **peseta** denominations.

USEFUL WORDS AND PHRASES

airmail	correo aéreo	*korreh-oh ah-aireh-oh*
ATM	el cajero automático	*kah-Heroh owtomateekoh*
bank	el banco	*bankoh*
bill, bank note	un billete de banco	*bee-yehteh deh bankoh*
cash	dinero en efectivo	*deeneroh en efekteevoh*
change (*verb*)	cambiar	*kambyar*
check	un cheque	*cheh-keh*
checkbook	el talonario de cheques	*talonaryoh deh cheh-kehss*
collection	la recogida	*reh-koh-Heeda*
counter	el mostrador	*mostra-dor*

credit card	la tarjeta de crédito	tar-Heh-ta deh kredeetoh
customs form	el impreso para la aduana	empreh-soh parra la adwah-na
delivery	el reparto	reh-partoh
deposit (noun)	un ingreso	eengreh-soh
(verb)	ingresar	eengreh-sar
dollar	el dólar	dohlar
exchange rate	el tipo de cambio	teepoh deh kambyoh
fax (noun)	un fax	fax
(verb: document)	mandar por fax	mandar por fax
fax machine	el fax	fax
form	un impreso	eempreh-soh
general delivery	la lista de correos	leesta deh korreh-oss
international money order	un giro internacional	Heeroh eentairnath-yonal
letter	una carta	karta
letter carrier	el cartero	karteh-roh
mail (noun)	el correo	korreh-oh
(verb)	echar al buzón	etchar al boothon
mailbox	el buzón	boothon
money order	un giro (postal)	Hee-roh postal
package/parcel	un paquete	pakeh-teh
postage rates	las tarifas postales	tarree-fass postah-less
postcard	una postal	postal
post office	(la oficina de) correos	offee-theena deh korreh-oss
registered letter	una carta certificada	karta thair-teefee-kah-da
stamp	un sello	say-yoh
surface mail	correo ordinario	korreh-oh ordee-nar-yoh
traveler's check	un cheque de viaje	cheh-keh deh vyah-Heh
withdraw	retirar/sacar	reteerar/sakar
withdrawal	una retirada	reteerah-da
zip code	el distrito	deestree-toh postal

How much is a letter/postcard to …
¿Qué franqueo lleva una carta/una postal a …
keh fran-keh-oh yeh-va oona karta/oona postal a

I would like three 45 peseta stamps
Quería tres sellos de cuarenta y cinco pesetas
keh-ree-a tress say-yoss deh kwarenti theenkoh pehseh-tass

I want to register this letter
Quiero mandar esta carta certificada
kee-eh-roh mandar esta karta thair-teefee-kah-da

I want to send this package to …
Quiero mandar este paquete a …
kee-eh-roh mandar esteh pakeh-teh a

How long does the mail to … take?
¿Cuánto tarda el correo para …?
kwantoh tarda el korreh-oh parra

Where can I mail this?
¿Dónde puedo echar esto?
dondeh pweh-doh etchar estoh

Is there any mail for me?
¿Hay algún correo para mí?
i algoon korreh-oh parra mee

I'd like to send a fax
Quería mandar un fax
keh-ree-a mandar oon fax

This is to go airmail
Esto quiero que vaya por avión
estoh kee-eh-roh keh va-ya por av-yon

I'd like to change this into pesetas
Quiero cambiar esto en pesetas
kee-eh-roh kambyar estoh en pehseh-tass

Can I cash these traveler's checks?
Quisiera hacer efectivos estos cheques de viaje
keesy<u>e</u>ra ath<u>ai</u>r efekt<u>ee</u>voss <u>e</u>stoss ch<u>eh</u>-kess deh vy<u>ah</u>-Heh

What is the exchange rate for the dollar?
¿A cuánto está el dólar?
a kw<u>a</u>ntoh est<u>a</u> el d<u>o</u>hlar

Can I draw cash using this credit card?
¿Puedo sacar dinero con esta tarjeta (de crédito)?
pw<u>eh</u>-doh sak<u>a</u>r deen<u>e</u>roh kon <u>e</u>sta tar-<u>Heh</u>-ta deh kr<u>e</u>deetoh

I'd like it in 5,000 peseta notes
¿Me lo puede dar en billetes de cinco mil, por favor?
meh loh pw<u>eh</u>-deh dar en bee-y<u>eh</u>-tess deh th<u>ee</u>nkoh meel por fa-v<u>o</u>r

Could you give me smaller bills?
¿Podría darme billetes más pequeños?
podr<u>ee</u>-a d<u>a</u>rmeh bee-y<u>eh</u>-tess mas peh-k<u>eh</u>-nyoss

---

THINGS YOU'LL SEE

banco	bank
buzón	mailbox
caja	cashier
cajero automático	ATM
cambio (de divisas)	currency exchange
cartas	letters
certificados	registered mail
correo aéreo	airmail
correo urgente	express
cuentas corrientes	checking accounts
destinatario	addressee
dirección	address
distrito postal	zip code
España	Spain (domestic postage)
extranjero	postage abroad

→

POST OFFICES AND BANKS

franqueo	postage
giros	money orders
horas de oficina	opening hours
horas de recogida	collection times
ingresos	deposits
lista de correos	general delivery
localidad	place
mercado de divisas	exchange rates
paquetes	packages
postal	postcard
rellenar	to fill in
remitente	sender
sello	stamp
tarifa	charge
venta de sellos	stamps

COMMUNICATIONS

Telephones: Telephone booths in Spain are blue. They take coins of 5, 25 and 100 pesetas as well as phonecards which are far more convenient and can be bought at newsstands and **estancos**. Some phones are equipped with multilingual electronic instruction displays.

To call the US, dial 07 and wait for a high-pitched tone, then dial 1 followed by the area code and the number you want.

The tones you hear on Spanish phones when making a call within Spain differ slightly from ours:

Dial tone:	same as in US
Ringing:	repeated long tone
Busy signal:	rapid beeps

There are also payphones in bars and restaurants, some of which have phones with a counter that is set to zero when you begin a call. Alternatively, you can look for the **central telefónica** or **teléfonos** (telephone exchange) that are located in the center of most towns. Run by **Telefónica** (look for the logo, standing for Spain's national telephone company), these are sometimes open 24 hours a day in major towns. You ask the cashier for the number you want, and then go to a booth and wait for the call to be put through. You pay when you have finished your call. Another sign to look for is **locutorio telefónico**, where you'll find telephone booths that operate the same system as the **central telefónica** and that are located near the beach in main resorts. There are also private **locutorios** in major towns which, although they can be more expensive, could save you a long trek to the **central telefónica**.

USEFUL WORDS AND PHRASES

call *(noun)*	una llamada	*yamah-da*
(verb)	llamar	*yamar*
cardphone	un teléfono con uso de tarjeta	*teh-leffonoh kon oosoh deh tar-Heh-ta*

code	el prefijo	*preh-fee-Hoh*
collect call	una llamada a cobro	*yamah-da a kobroh*
	revertido	*reh-vair-teedoh*
dial	marcar	*markar*
dial tone	la señal para marcar	*sen-yal parra markar*
email address	la dirección de email	*deerektheeon deh*
		eemail
emergency	una emergencia	*emmair-Henth-ya*
extension	extensión	*ekstenth-yon*
fax machine	el fax	*fax*
information	información	*eenformath-yon*
internet	el internet	*internet*
international	internacional	*eentair-nath-yonal*
mobile phone	el teléfono móvil	*teh-leffonoh mohbeel*
number	el número	*noomeh-roh*
operator	la operadora	*opeh-radora*
payphone	un teléfono público	*teh-leffonoh*
		poobleekoh
phone booth	una cabina	*kabeena*
	telefónica	*tehleh-fonnika*
phonecard	una tarjeta de	*tar-Heh-ta deh*
	teléfono	*teh-leffonoh*
phone book	la guía telefónica	*gee-a tehleh-fonnika*
photocopier	la fotocopiadora	*fotokopeeadora*
receiver	el aparato	*aparah-toh*
telephone	un teléfono	*teh-leffonoh*
touch-tone	un teléfono	*teh-leffonoh*
phone	automático	*owtoh-matikoh*
website	la web site	*'web site'*
wrong number	el número	*noomeh-roh*
	equivocado	*eh-keevoh-kah-doh*

Where is the nearest phone booth?
¿Dónde está la cabina telefónica más cercana?
dondeh esta la kabeena tehleh-fonnika mass thair-kah-na

Is there a phone book?
¿Hay una guía telefónica?
I oona gee-a tehleh-fonnika

How much is a call to America?
¿Cuánto cuesta una llamada a América?
kwantoh kwesta oona yamah-da a amairika

I would like to make a collect call
Quiero que sea a cobro revertido
kyeh-roh keh seh-a a koh-broh reh-vair-teedoh

I would like a number in Barcelona
Quiero un número de Barcelona
kyeh-roh oon noomeh-roh deh bartheh-lohna

Could you give me an outside line?
¿Puede darme línea, por favor?
pweh-deh dar-meh leeneh-a por fa-vor

How do I get an outside line?
¿Cómo puedo obtener línea?
koh-moh pweh-doh obtenair leeneh-a

Hello, this is … speaking
Hola, soy …
oh-la soy

Is that …?
¿Es (usted) …?
ess oosteh

Hello (when answering)
Dígame
dee-gah-meh

Speaking
Al habla
al abla

COMMUNICATIONS

I would like to speak to …
Quería hablar con …
keh-ree-a ablar kon

Extension …, please
Extensión …, por favor
ekstenss-yon … por fa-vor

Please tell him/her … called
Haga el favor de decirle que ha llamado …
ah-ga el fa-vor deh deh-theerleh keh a yamah-doh

Would you ask him/her to call me back, please
Dígale que me llame cuando vuelva
dee-gah-leh keh meh yah-meh kwandoh vwelva

Do you know where he/she is?
¿Sabe usted dónde está?
sah-beh oosteh dondeh esta

When will he/she be back?
¿Cuándo volverá?
kwandoh volveh-ra

Could you leave him/her a message?
¿Podría dejarle un recado?
podree-a deh-Harleh oon reh-kah-doh

I'll call back later
Volveré a llamar luego
volveh-reh a yamar lweh-goh

Sorry, I've got the wrong number
Lo siento, me he equivocado de número
loh syen-toh meh eh ekeevoh-kah-doh deh noomeh-roh

What's your fax number/email address?
¿Cual es su número de fax/dirección de email?
kwal ess soo noomeh-roh deh fax/deerektheeon de eemail

Did you get my fax/email?
¿Recibió mi fax/email?
retheebee__oh__ mee fax/eemail

Please resend your fax
Por favor, envíe de nuevo su fax
por fav__or__ enb__ee__-eh de noo__e__bo soo fax

Can I use the photocopier/fax machine?
¿Puedo usar la fotocopiadora/el fax
pw__eh__-doh oos__ar__ la fotokopeead__or__a/el fax

THE ALPHABET

a	*ah*	g	*Heh*	n	*eneh*	t	*teh*
b	*beh*	h	*acheh*	ñ	*enyeh*	u	*oo*
c	*theh*	i	*ee*	o	*o*	v	*oobeh*
ch	*cheh*	j	*Hota*	p	*peh*	w	*oobeh dobleh*
d	*deh*	k	*ka*	q	*koo*	x	*ekiss*
e	*eh*	l	*eleh*	r	*ereh*	y	*ee gryehga*
f	*efeh*	m	*emeh*	s	*eseh*	z	*thehta*

THINGS YOU'LL SEE

cabina telefónica	telephone booth
central telefónica	telephone exchange
descolgar el aparato	lift receiver
Estados Unidos (EEUU)	US
fax	fax machine
fotocopiadora	photocopier
guía telefónica	telephone book
insertar monedas	insert coins
interurbana	long-distance
llamada	call
locutorio telefónico	telephone booth

→

marcar el número	dial the number
monedas	coins
no funciona	out of order
número	number
operadora	operator
páginas amarillas	Yellow Pages
paso (de contador)	unit
prefijo	area code
reparaciones	repair service
servicio a través de operadora	dialing through the operator
servicio automático	direct dialing
sitio web	website
tarifa	charges
tarjeta telefónica	phonecard
Telefónica	Spanish national telephone company
teléfono móvil	mobile phone
urbana	local
web site	website

THINGS YOU'LL HEAR

¿A dónde quiere llamar?
Where do you want to call?

Vaya a la cabina cuatro
Now go to booth number 4

¿Con quién quiere que le ponga?
Whom would you like to speak to?

Se ha equivocado de número
You've got the wrong number

¿Quién es?
Who's speaking?

→

Al aparato/Al habla/Soy yo
Speaking

Diga/Dígame
Hello

¿Cuál es su teléfono?
What is your number?

Lo siento, no está
Sorry, he/she's not in

Puede dejar un recado
You can leave a message

Volverá dentro de … minutos/horas
He'll/she'll be back in … minutes/hours

Vuelva a llamar mañana, por favor
Please call again tomorrow

Le diré que le/la ha llamado usted
I'll tell him/her you called

**Las líneas con Sevilla se encuentran ocupadas en este
momento. Repita la llamada dentro de unos minutos.**
All lines to Seville are busy at the moment. Please call again in
a few minutes' time.

Le pongo/paso con …
I'll put you through…

EMERGENCIES

Information on local health services can be obtained from
tourist information offices, but in an emergency dial **091** for
the police. They will put you through to the ambulance service
or fire department, since there is no national central number
for these emergency services.

In case of sudden illness or accident, go to the nearest **casa
de socorro** (emergency first-aid center) or to an **urgencias**
(hospital emergency room). If on the road, look for **puestos
de socorro**, which is also an emergency first-aid center.

In the event of your car breaking down, try to get to the
nearest **taller** (garage) or, if this is not possible, to the nearest
service station, where they will be able to advise you on whom
to phone. If you are a member of AAA, there is a reciprocal
agreement with the **RACE** (**Real Automóvil Club de España**)
under which you should be covered.

USEFUL WORDS AND PHRASES

accident	un accidente	*akthee-denteh*
ambulance	una ambulancia	*amboolanth-ya*
assault	agredir	*agreh-deer*
breakdown	una avería	*aveh-ree-a*
break down (*verb*)	tener una avería	*tenair oona aveh-ree-a*
burglar	un ladrón	*ladron*
burglary	un robo	*roh-boh*
crash	un accidente	*akthee-denteh*
emergency	una emergencia	*emair-Henth-ya*
emergency room	urgencias	*oor-Henth-yass*
fire	un fuego	*fwehgoh*
(*large*)	un incendio	*eenthend-yoh*
fire department	los bomberos	*bombeh-ross*
flood	una inundación	*eenoondath-yon*
injured	herido	*ereedoh*
pickpocket	un carterista	*kartereesta*

police	la policía	*poleethee-a*
police station	la comisaria	*kommeessaree-a*
theft	un robo	*rohboh*
thief	un ladrón	*ladron*
tow	remolcar	*remolkar*
towing service	servicio de grúa	*saitveeth yoh deh groo-a*

Help!
¡Socorro!
sokorroh

Look out!
¡Cuidado!
kweedah-doh

Stop!
¡Pare!
pareh

This is an emergency!
¡Esto es una emergencia!
estoh ess oona emair-Henth-ya

Get an ambulance!
¡Llame a una ambulancia!
yah-meh a oona amboolanth-ya

Hurry up!
¡Dése prisa!
deh-seh preessa

Please send an ambulance to …
Mande una ambulancia a …
mandeh oona amboolanth-ya a

Please come to …
Haga el favor de venir a …
ah-ga el fa-vor deh veneer a

My address is …
Mi dirección es …
mee deerekth-yon ess

We've had a break-in
Hemos tenido un robo en la casa
ehmoss teneedoh oon rohboh en la kasa

There's a fire at …
Hay un fuego en …
I oon fwehgoh en

Someone's been injured/run over
Hay una persona herida/atropellada
I oona pairsona ereeda/atropeh-yah-da

He's passed out
Ha perdido el conocimiento
a pairdeedoh el konotheemmyentoh

My passport/car has been stolen
Me han robado el pasaporte/el coche
meh an robah-doh el passaporteh/el kotcheh

I've lost my traveler's checks
He perdido mis cheques de viaje
eh pairdeedoh meess cheh-kess deh vyah-Heh

I want to report a stolen credit card
Quiero denunciar el robo de una tarjeta de crédito
kyeh-roh denoonthyar el rohboh deh oona tar-Heh-ta deh kredeetoh

It was stolen from my room
Lo robaron de mi habitación
lo robah-ron deh mee abeetath-yon

I lost it in/at…
Lo perdí en …
lo pairdee en

My luggage is missing
Mi equipaje se ha perdido
mee ekeep<u>ah</u>-Heh seh a paird<u>ee</u>doh

Has my luggage turned up yet?
¿Ha aparecido ya mi equipaje?
a apareh-th<u>ee</u>doh ya mee ekeep<u>ah</u>-Heh

I've had a crash
He tenido un accidente
eh ten<u>ee</u>doh oon akthee-d<u>e</u>nteh

My car's been broken into
Me han forzado el coche
meh an forth<u>ah</u>-doh el k<u>o</u>tcheh

The registration number is …
El número de matrícula es el …
el n<u>oo</u>meroh deh matr<u>ee</u>koola ess el

I've been mugged
Me han atacado
meh an atak<u>ah</u>-doh

My son's missing
Mi hijo se ha perdido
mee <u>ee</u>-Hoh seh a paird<u>ee</u>edo

He has fair/brown hair
Tiene el pelo rubio/moreno
ty<u>e</u>h-neh el p<u>e</u>h-loh r<u>oo</u>b-yoh/mor<u>e</u>h-noh

He's … years old
Tiene … años
ty<u>e</u>h-neh … <u>ah</u>n-yoss

I've locked myself out of my house/room/car
Me he dejado la llave dentro de la casa/habitación/del coche
*meh eh deh-H<u>ah</u>-doh la y<u>ah</u>-veh d<u>e</u>ntroh deh la k<u>a</u>sa/abeetath-y<u>o</u>n/
  del k<u>o</u>tcheh*

EMERGENCIES

He's drowning
Se está ahogando
seh esta ah-oh-gandoh

She can't swim
No sabe nadar
noh sabeh nadar

THINGS YOU'LL SEE

abierto las 24 horas del día	24-hour service
botiquín	first-aid box
casa de socorro	emergency first-aid center
comisaría	police station
farmacia de guardia	pharmacy on duty
fuego	fire
guardia civil de tráfico	traffic police
marque …	dial …
policía	police
primeros auxilios	first-aid center
puesto de socorro	first-aid center
servicios de rescate	mountain rescue
socorrista	lifeguard
taller (de reparaciones)	garage
urgencias	emergency room

THINGS YOU'LL HEAR

¿Cuál es su dirección?
What's your address?

¿Dónde se encuentra usted ahora?
Where are you?

¿Puede describirlo/describirle?
Can you describe it/him?

HEALTH

Medicines are available only from the **farmacia** (pharmacy),
usually open from 9 AM to 1 PM and from 4 PM to 8 PM. If the
pharmacy is closed, there will be a notice on the door that gives
the address of the **farmacia de guardia**—pharmacy on duty
(See Emergencies, page 108.)

USEFUL WORDS AND PHRASES

accident	un accidente	*akthee-denteh*
ambulance	una ambulancia	*amboolanth-ya*
anemic	anémico	*anneh-meekoh*
appendicitis	una apendicitis	*apendee-theeteess*
appendix	el apéndice	*apen-deetheh*
aspirin	una aspirina	*asspee-reena*
asthma	asma	*azma*
backache	un dolor de espalda	*dolor deh esspalda*
bandage	el vendaje	*vendah-Heh*
bite (by dog)	una mordedura	*mordeh-doora*
(by insect)	una picadura	*peeka-doora*
bladder	la vejiga	*veh-Heega*
blister	una ampolla	*ampoh-ya*
blood	la sangre	*sangreh*
blood donor	un donante de sangre	*doh-nanteh deh sangreh*
burn	una quemadura	*keh-madoora*
cancer	el cáncer	*kanthair*
cast	la escayola	*eskayyoh-la*
chest	el pecho	*peh-tchoh*
chicken pox	la varicela	*varee-theh-la*
cold	un resfriado	*resfree-ah-doh*
concussion	una conmoción	*konmth-yon*
constipation	estreñimiento	*estren-yeem-yentoh*
contact lenses	las lentes de contacto	*lentess deh kontaktoh*

113

corn	un callo	k<u>a</u>h-yoh
cough	tos	toss
cut	un corte	korteh
dentist	el dentista	dent<u>ee</u>sta
diabetes	la diabetes	dee-ab<u>eh</u>--tess
diarrhea	una diarrea	dee-arr<u>eh</u>-a
dizzy	mareado	marreh-<u>ah</u>-doh
doctor	el médico	m<u>e</u>ddeekoh
earache	un dolor de oídos	dolor deh oh-<u>ee</u>doss
fever	la fiebre	fee-<u>eh</u>-breh
filling	un empaste	emp<u>a</u>steh
first aid	primeros auxilios	preem<u>eh</u>-ross owk-z<u>ee</u>l-yoss
flu	la gripe	gr<u>ee</u>peh
fracture	una fractura	frakt<u>oo</u>ra
German measles	la rubeola	roobeh-<u>o</u>la
glasses	las gafas	g<u>a</u>h-fass
hangover	una resaca	res<u>a</u>ka
hay fever	la fiebre del heno	fee-<u>eh</u>-breh del <u>eh</u>-noh
headache	un dolor de cabeza	dolor deh kab<u>eh</u>-tha
heart	el corazón	korrath<u>o</u>n
heart attack	un infarto	eemf<u>a</u>rtoh
hemorrhage	una hemorragia	emmoraH-hya
hepatitis	la hepatitis	hehpat<u>ee</u>tees
HIV positive	seropositivo	sehrroposeet<u>ee</u>veh
hospital	el hospital	osspeet<u>a</u>l
indigestion	una indigestión	eendee-Hest-y<u>o</u>n
injection	una inyección	eenyekth-y<u>o</u>n
itch	un picor	peek<u>o</u>r
kidney	el riñón	reen-y<u>o</u>n
lump	un bulto	b<u>oo</u>ltoh
measles	el sarampión	saramp-y<u>o</u>n
migraine	una jaqueca	Hak<u>eh</u>-ka
motion sickness sickness	mareo	marr<u>eh</u>-oh

mumps	las paperas	*papeh-rass*
nausea	náuseas	*now-seh-ass*
nurse *(female)*	la enfermera	*enfairmeh-ra*
(male)	el enfermero	*ennfairmeh-ro*
operation	una operación	*oppeh-rath-yon*
optician	el oculista	*okooleess-ta*
pain	un dolor	*dolor*
penicillin	la penicilina	*peneethee-leena*
pharmacy	la farmacia	*farmath-ya*
pneumonia	una neumonía	*neh-oomonee-a*
pregnant	embarazada	*embarra-thah-da*
prescription	una receta	*reh-theh-ta*
rheumatism	el reúma	*reh-oo-ma*
scald	una quemadura	*keh-madoora*
scratch	un arañazo	*arran-yah-thoh*
sick	enfermo	*emfairmoh*
sore throat	un dolor de garganta	*dolor deh garganta*
splinter	una astilla	*astee-ya*
sprain	una torcedura	*tortheh-doora*
sting	una picadura	*peeka-doora*
stomach	el estómago	*estoh-magoh*
tonsils	las amígdalas	*ameegda-lass*
toothache	un dolor de muelas	*dolor deh mweh-lass*
ulcer	una úlcera	*ooltheh-ra*
vaccination	la vacunación	*vakoonath-yon*
vomit	vomitar	*vommee-tar*
whooping cough	la tosferina	*tossfeh-reena*

I have a pain in …
Me duele …
meh dweh-leh

I don't feel well
No me encuentro bien
noh men enkwen-troh byen

I feel faint
Me encuentro débil
meh enkwen-troh-deh-beel

I feel sick
Tengo náuseas
teng-goh now-seh-ass

I feel dizzy
Estoy mareado
estoy marreh-ah-doh

It hurts here
Me duele aquí
meh dweh-leh akee

It's a sharp pain
Es un dolor agudo
ess oon dolor agoodoh

It's a dull pain
Es un dolor leve
ess oon dolor lehve

It hurts all the time
Es un dolor constante
ess oon dolor konstanteh

It only hurts now and then
Sólo me duele a ratos
soloh meh dweh-leh a rah-toss

It hurts when you touch it
Me duele al tocarlo
meh dweh-leh al tokarloh

It hurts more at night
Me duele más por la noche
meh dweh-leh mass por la notcheh

It stings/It itches
Me escuece/Me pica
meh ess-kw_eh_-theh/meh p_ee_ka

It aches
Me duele
meh dw_eh_-leh

I have a temperature
Tengo fiebre
t_e_ng-goh fee-_eh_-breh

I'm ... months pregnant
Estoy embarrazada de ... meses
est_oy_ embarrath_a_hda de ... mehses

I need a prescription for ...
Necesito una receta para ...
nehtheh-s_ee_toh _oo_na reh-th_eh_-ta parra

Can you take these if you are pregnant/breastfeeding?
¿Se puede tomar esto estando embarazada/dando el pecho?
seh pw_eh_de tohmar _e_stoh estandoh embarrath_a_hda/d_a_hndo el p_eh_-tchoh

I normally take ...
Normalmente tomo ...
normalm_e_nteh t_oh_-moh

I'm allergic to ...
Soy alérgico a ...
soy all_ai_r-Heekoh a

Have you got anything for ...?
¿Tiene usted algo para ...?
ty_eh_-neh oost_eh_ _a_lgoh p_a_rra

Do I need a prescription for ...?
¿Hace falta receta para ...?
_ah_-theh f_a_lta reh-th_eh_-ta p_a_rra

HEALTH

I have lost a filling
Se me ha caído un empaste
seh meh a ka-_ee_doh oon emp_a_steh

Will he/she be all right?
¿Estará bien?
estar_a_ byen

Will he/she need an operation?
¿Va a necesitar una operación?
ba a nethessee-t_a_r _oo_na oppeh-rath-y_o_n

How is she/he?
¿Cómo está?
*k_oh_-moh est_a_*

THINGS YOU'LL SEE

análisis clínicos	clinical tests
casa de socorro	first-aid center
clínica dental	dentist's office
consulta	doctor's office
farmacia de guardia	pharmacy on duty
ginecólogo	gynecologist
médico	doctor
médico general	General Practitioner
oculista	optician
otorrinolaringólogo	ear, nose, and throat specialist
pediatra	pediatrician
primeros auxilios	first-aid center
sala de espera	waiting room
test del embarazo	pregnancy test
tomamos la tensión	take your blood pressure
urgencias	emergencies

118

THINGS YOU'LL HEAR

Tome usted ... comprimidos/pastillas cada vez
Take ... pills/tablets at a time

Con agua
With water

Mastíquelos
Chew them

Una vez/dos veces/tres veces al día
Once/twice/three times a day

Al acostarse
When you go to bed

¿Qué toma normalmente?
What do you normally take?

Debería consultar a un médico
I think you should see a doctor

Lo siento, no lo tenemos
I'm sorry, we don't have that

Hace falta una receta médica para eso
You need a prescription for that

CONVERSION TABLES

DISTANCES

A mile is 1.6km. To convert kilometers to miles, divide the km by 8 and multiply by 5. Convert miles to km by dividing the miles by 5 and multiplying by 8.

miles	0.62	1.24	1.86	2.43	3.11	3.73	4.35	6.21
miles *or* **km**	1	2	3	4	5	6	7	10
km	1.61	3.22	4.83	6.44	8.05	9.66	11.27	16.10

WEIGHTS

The kilogram is equivalent to 2lb 3oz. To convert kg to lbs, divide by 5 and multiply by 11. One ounce is about 28 grams, and 8 oz about 227 grams; 1lb is therefore about 454 grams.

lbs	2.20	4.41	6.61	8.82	11.02	13.23	19.84	22.04
lbs *or* **kg**	1	2	3	4	5	6	9	10
kg	0.45	0.91	1.36	1.81	2.27	2.72	4.08	4.53

TEMPERATURE

To convert degrees Celsius into Fahrenheit, the accurate method is to multiply the C° figure by 1.8 and add 32. Similarly, to convert F° to C°, subtract 32 from the F° figure and divide by 1.8.

C°	-10	0	5	10	20	30	36.9	40	100
F°	14	32	41	50	68	86	98.4	104	212

LIQUIDS

A liter is about 0.53 pints; a gallon is roughly 3.8 liters.

gals	0.27	0.53	1.33	2.65	5.31	7.96	13.26
gals *or* **liters**	1	2	5	10	20	30	50
liters	3.77	7.54	18.85	37.70	75.40	113.10	188.50

TIRE PRESSURES

lb/sq in	18	20	22	24	26	28	30	33
kg/sq cm	1.3	1.4	1.5	1.7	1.8	2.0	2.1	2.3

MINI-DICTIONARY

Where two forms of nouns or pronouns are given in the Spanish, the first is masculine and the second feminine; e.g. "they" **ellos/ellas**, "this one" **éste/ésta**.

There are two verbs "to be" in Spanish: **ser** is used to describe a permanent condition, such as nationality and occupation, and **estar** is used to describe a temporary condition. Both forms are given in this order in the dictionary.

a un/una *(see p 5)*
about: about 16 alrededor de dieciséis
accelerator el acelerador
accident el accidente
accommodations el alojamiento
ache el dolor
adaptor el adaptador
address la dirección
adhesive el pegamento
admission charge el precio de entrada
after ... después de ...
aftershave el after-shave
again otra vez
against contra
agency la agencia
AIDS el Sida
air el aire
air conditioning el aire acondicionado
aircraft el avión
airline la compañía aérea
airport el aeropuerto
airport bus el autobús del aeropuerto
aisle el pasillo
alarm clock el despertador
alcohol el alcohol
Algeria Argelia
all todo
   all the streets todas las calles
   that's all eso es todo
almost casi

alone solo
already ya
always siempre
am: I am soy/estoy
ambulance la ambulancia
America América
American *(man)* el americano
   (woman) la americana
   (adj.) americano
and y; *(before word beginning with "i" or "hi")* e
ankle el tobillo
another otro
answering machine el contestador automático
antifreeze el anticongelante
antiseptic el antiséptico
apartment el apartamento, el piso
aperitif el aperitivo
appetite el apetito
apple la manzana
application form el impreso de solicitud
appointment *(business)* la cita
   (at hair salon) hora
apricot el albaricoque
are: you are es/está
   (familiar) eres/estás
   we are somos/estamos
   they are son/están
arm el brazo

arrive llegar
art el arte
art gallery la galería de arte
artist el/la artista
as: as soon as possible lo antes posible
ashtray el cenicero
asleep: he's asleep está dormido
aspirin la aspirina
at: at the post office en Correos
  at night por la noche
  at 3 o'clock a las tres
ATM el cajero automático
ATM card la tarjeta de banco
Atlantic Ocean el Océano Atlántico
attractive (person) guapo
  (object) bonito
  (offer) atractivo
aunt la tía
Australia Australia
Australian (man) el australiano
  (woman) la australiana
  (adj.) australiano
auto-body shop el taller
automatic automático
away: is it far away? ¿está lejos?
  go away! ¡váyase!
awful horrible
ax el hacha
axle el eje

baby el niño pequeño, el bebé
baby carriage el cochecito
baby wipes las toallitas para bebé
back (not front) la parte de atrás
  (body) la espalda
  to come back volver
backpack la mochila
bacon el bacon
  bacon and eggs huevos fritos
  con bacon
bad malo
bag la bolsa
bait el cebo
bake cocer al horno

bakery la panadería
balcony el balcón
Balearic Islands las (Islas) Baleares
ball la pelota
ballpoint pen el bolígrafo
banana el plátano
band (musicians) la banda
bandage la venda
bangs (hair) el flequillo
bank el banco
bar (drinks) el bar
  bar of chocolate una tableta de
  chocolate
barbecue la barbacoa
barber's la peluquería de caballeros
bargain la ganga
basement el sótano
basin (sink) el lavabo
basket el cesto
bath el baño
  to take a bath darse un baño
bathing suit el bañador,
  el traje de baño
bathroom el cuarto de baño
battery (car) la batería
  (flashlight, etc.) la pila
Bay of Biscay el Golfo de Vizcaya
beach la playa
beach ball el balón de playa
beans las judías
beard la barba
beautiful (object) precioso
  (person) guapo
because porque
bed la cama
bed linen la ropa de cama
bedroom el dormitorio
beef la carne de vaca
beer la cerveza
before ... antes de ...
beginner un/una principiante
behind ... detrás de ...
beige beige
bell (church) la campana
  (door) el timbre

below ... debajo de ...
belt el cinturón
beside al lado de
best (el) mejor
better mejor
between ... entre ...
bicycle la bicicleta
big grande
bill la cuenta
  (*money*) el billete de banco
bird el pájaro
birthday el cumpleaños
  happy birthday! ¡felicidades!
birthday present
  el regalo de cumpleaños
bite (*noun: by dog*) la mordedura
  (*by insect*) la picadura
  (*verb: by dog*) morder
  (*by insect*) picar
bitter amargo
black negro
blackberries las moras
blackcurrants las grosellas negras
blanket la manta
bleach (*noun*) la lejía
  (*verb: hair*) teñir
blind (*cannot see*) ciego
blinds las persianas
blister una ampolla
blizzard la ventisca
blond(e) (*adj.*) rubio
blood la sangre
blouse la blusa
blue azul
boat el barco
  (*small*) la barca
body el cuerpo
boil (*of water*) hervir
  (*egg, etc.*) cocer
bolt (*noun: on door*) el cerrojo
  (*verb*) echar el cerrojo
bone el hueso
book (*noun*) el libro
  (*verb*) reservar
bookstore la librería

boot la bota
border el borde
  (*between countries*) la frontera
boring aburrido
born: I was born in ...
  nací en ...
both: both of them los dos
  both of us los dos
  both ... **and** ...
  tanto ... como ...
bottle la botella
bottle opener el abrebotellas
bottom el fondo
  (*part of body*) el trasero
bowl el cuenco
box la caja
box office la taquilla
boy el chico
boyfriend el novio
bra el sostén
bracelet la pulsera
braces los tirantes
brake (*noun*) el freno
  (*verb*) frenar
brandy el coñac
bread el pan
breakdown (*car*) la avería
  (*nervous*) la crisis nerviosa
  I've had a breakdown (*car*)
  he tenido una avería
breakfast el desayuno
breathe respirar
bridge el puente
  (*game*) el bridge
briefcase la cartera
British británico
brochure el folleto
broiler la parrilla
broken roto
brooch el broche
brother el hermano
brown marrón
  (*hair*) castaño
  (*skin*) moreno
bruise el cardenal

brush (noun: hair) el cepillo del pelo
(paint) la brocha
(for cleaning) el cepillo
(verb: hair) cepillar el pelo
bucket el cubo
building el edificio
bull el toro
bullfight la corrida de toros
bullfighter el torero
bullring la plaza de toros
bumper el parachoques
burglar el ladrón
burn (noun) la quemadura
(verb) quemar
bus el autobús
(long-distance) el autobús
business el negocio
  it's none of your business no es asunto suyo
bus station la estación de autobuses
busy (occupied) ocupado
(bar) concurrido
but pero
butcher's la carnicería
butter la mantequilla
button el botón
buy comprar
by: by the window junto a la ventana
  by Friday para el viernes
  by myself yo solo
  written by ... escrito por ...

cabbage la col
cabinet el armario
cable car el teleférico
cable TV la television por cable
café el café
cake (small) el pastel
(large) la tarta
  sponge cake el bizcocho
calculator la calculadora
call: what's it called? ¿cómo se llama?
camcorder la videocámara
camera la máquina de fotos

campsite el camping
camshaft el árbol de levas
can: can you ...? ¿puede ...?
  I can't ... no puedo ...
can (tin) la lata
Canada Canadá
Canadian el/la canadiense
(adj.) canadiense
canal el canal
Canaries las (Islas) Canarias
candle la vela
candy el caramelo
can opener el abrelatas
cap (bottle) el tapón
(hat) la gorra
car el coche
(train) el vagón
carbonated con gas
carburetor el carburador
card la tarjeta
cardigan la rebeca
careful prudente
  be careful! ¡cuidado!
caretaker el portero, el encargado
carpet la alfombra
carrot la zanahoria
car seat (for a baby/child) el asiento
  infantil
case (suitcase) la maleta
cash (noun) el dinero
(verb) cobrar
  to pay cash pagar al contado
cassette la cassette, la cinta
cassette player el cassette
castanets unas castañuelas
Castile Castilla
Castilian el castellano
castle el castillo
cat el gato
Catalonia Cataluña
cathedral la catedral
Catholic (adj.) católico
cauliflower la coliflor
cave la cueva
cemetery el cementerio

center el centro
central heating la calefacción central
certificate el certificado
chair la silla
change (noun: money) el cambio
  (verb: money) cambiar
  (clothes) cambiarse
  (trains, etc.) hacer transbordo
check (noun) el cheque
checkbook el talonario de cheques
check-in (desk) (el mostrador de)
  facturación
check in (verb) facturar
cheers! (toast) ¡salud!
cheese el queso
cherry la cereza
chess el adjedrez
chest (part of body) el pecho
  (furniture) el arcón
chest of drawers la cómoda
chewing gum el chicle
chicken el pollo
child el niño
  (female) la niña
children los niños
china la porcelana
chocolate el chocolate
  box of chocolates una caja de
  bombones
chop (food) la chuleta
  (verb: cut) cortar
church la iglesia
cigar el puro
cigarette el cigarrillo
cinema el cine
city la ciudad
city center el centro (urbano)
class la clase
classical music
  la música clásica
clean (adj.) limpio
clear (obvious) evidente
  (water) claro
clever listo
clock el reloj

close (near) cerca
  (stuffy) sofocante
  (verb) cerrar
closed cerrado
clothes la ropa
clubs (cards) tréboles
coat el abrigo
coat hanger la percha
cockroach la cucaracha
coffee el café
coin la moneda
cold (illness) un resfriado
  (adj.) frío
  I have a cold tengo un resfriado
  I am cold tengo frío
collar el cuello
  (of animal) el collar
collection (stamps, etc.) la colección
  (postal) la recogida
color el color
color film la película en color
comb (noun) el peine
  (verb) peinar
come venir
  I come from ... soy de ...
  we came last week llegamos la
  semana pasada
  come here! ¡venga aquí!
comforter el edredón
compact disk el disco compacto
compartment el compartimento
complicated complicado
computer el ordenador
concert el concierto
conditioner (hair) el acondicionador
condom el condón
conductor (bus) el cobrador
  (orchestra) el director
congratulations! ¡enhorabuena!
consulate el consulado
contact lenses las lentes de contacto
contraceptive el anticonceptivo
cook (noun) el cocinero
  (female) la cocinera
  (verb) guisar

cookie la galleta
cooking utensils los utensilios de cocina
cool fresco
cork el corcho
corkscrew el sacacorchos
corner *(of street)* la esquina
  (of room) el rincón
corridor el pasillo
cosmetics los cosméticos
cost *(verb)* costar
  what does it cost? ¿cuánto cuesta?
cotton el algodón
cotton balls el algodón
cough *(noun)* la tos
  (verb) toser
cough drops las pastillas para la garganta
country *(state)* el país
  (not town) el campo
cousin el primo
  (female) la prima
crab el cangrejo
cramp el calambre
crayfish las cigalas
cream *(dairy)* la nata
  (lotion) la crema
credit card la tarjeta de crédito
crib el capazo
crowded lleno
cruise el crucero
crutches las muletas
cry *(weep)* llorar
  (shout) gritar
cucumber el pepino
cuff links los gemelos
cup la taza
curlers los rulos
curls los rizos
curry el curry
curtain la cortina
customs la aduana
cut *(noun)* la cortadura
  (verb) cortar

dad papá
damp húmedo
dance *(noun)* el baile
  (verb) bailar
dangerous peligroso
dark oscuro
  dark blue azul oscuro
daughter la hija
day el día
dead muerto
deaf sordo
dear *(person)* querido
deck of cards la baraja
deep profundo
delayed retrasado
deliberately a propósito
dentist el/la dentista
dentures la dentadura postiza
deny negar
deodorant el desodorante
department store los grandes almacenes
departure la salida
departure lounge salidas
develop *(film)* revelar
diamonds *(jewels)* los diamantes
  (cards) diamantes
diaper el pañal
diarrhea la diarrea
diary la agenda
dictionary el diccionario
die morir
diesel *(oil)* fuel-oil
  (adj.: engine) diesel
different diferente
  that's different! ¡eso es distinto!
  I'd like a different one quería otro distinto
difficult difícil
dining room el comedor
dirty sucio
disabled minusválido
dish cloth el paño de cocina
dishwashing detergent el lavavajillas
disposable diapers pañales desechables
distributor *(car)* el distribuidor

divorced divorciado
do hacer
　how do you do? ¿qué tal?
dock el muelle
doctor el médico
　(female) la médica
document el documento
dog el perro
doll la muñeca
dollar el dólar
door la puerta
double room la habitación doble
doughnut el dónut®
down hacia abajo
dress el vestido
drink *(noun)* la bebida
　(verb) beber
　would you like a drink? ¿quiere
　beber algo?
drinking water agua potable
drive *(verb)* conducir
driver el conductor
driving regulations el código de la
　circulación
driver's license el carnet de conducir
drunk borracho
dry seco
　(sherry) fino
during durante
dust cloth el trapo del polvo
duty-free libre de impuestos
　duty-free shop el duty-free

each *(every)* cada
　300 pesetas each trescientas pesetas
　cada uno
ear *(inner)* el oído
　(outer) la oreja
　ears las orejas
early temprano
earrings los pendientes
east el Este
easy fácil
eat comer

egg el huevo
either: either of them cualquiera de ellos
　either … or … o bien … o …
elastic elástico
elbow el codo
electric eléctrico
electricity la electricidad
elevator el ascensor
else: something else algo más
　someone else alguien más
　somewhere else en otro sitio
email el email
email address la dirección de email
embarrassing embarazoso
embassy la embajada
embroidery el bordado
emergency la emergencia
emergency brake *(train)* el freno de
　emergencia
emergency exit la salida de emergencia
empty vacío
end el final
engaged *(couple)* prometido
engine *(motor)* el motor
England Inglaterra
English inglés
Englishman el inglés
Englishwoman la inglesa
enlargement la ampliación
enough bastante
entertainment las diversiones
entrance la entrada
envelope el sobre
eraser la goma de borrar
escalator la escalera mecánica
especially sobre todo
evening la tarde
every cada
　every day todos los días
everyone todos
everything todo
everywhere por todas partes
example el ejemplo
　for example por ejemplo
excellent excelente

excess baggage exceso de equipaje
exchange (*verb*) cambiar
exchange rate el cambio
excursion la excursión
excuse me! (*to get attention*) ¡oiga,
  por favor!
  (*when sneezing, etc.*) ¡perdón!
  excuse me, please (*to get past*)
  ¿me hace el favor?
exit la salida
expensive caro
extension cord el cable alargador
eye el ojo

face la cara
faint (*unclear*) tenue
  (*verb*) desmayarse
fair (*noun*) la feria
  it's not fair no hay derecho
false teeth la dentadura postiza
family la familia
fan (*ventilator*) el ventilador
  (*handheld*) el abanico
  (*enthusiast*) el fan
  (*football*) el hincha
fantastic fantástico
far lejos
  how far is it to …?
  ¿qué distancia hay a …?
fare el billete
farm la granja
farmer el granjero
fashion la moda
fast rápido
fat (*person*) gordo
  (*on meat, etc.*) la grasa
father el padre
faucet el grifo
fax (*noun*) el fax
  (*verb: document*) enviar por fax
feel (*touch*) tocar
  I feel hot tengo calor
  I feel like … me apetece …
  I don't feel well no me encuentro bien

felt-tip pen el rotulador
fence la cerca
ferry el ferry
fiancé el prometido
fiancée la prometida
field el campo
fig el higo
filling (*in tooth*) el empaste
  (*in sandwich, cake*) el relleno
film la película
filter el filtro
filter papers los papeles de filtro
finger el dedo
fire el fuego
  (*blaze*) el incendio
fire extinguisher el extintor
fireworks los fuegos artificiales
first primero
  first aid primeros auxilios
first name el nombre de pila
fish el pez
  (*food*) el pescado
fishing la pesca
  to go fishing ir a pescar
fish market la pescadería
flag la bandera
flash (*camera*) el flash
flashlight la linterna
flat (*level*) plano
flavor el sabor
flea la pulga
flight el vuelo
floor el suelo
  (*story*) el piso
flour la harina
flower la flor
flute la flauta
fly (*insect*) la mosca
  (*verb: of plane, insect*) volar
  (*of person*) viajar en avión
fog la niebla
folk music la música folklórica
food la comida
food poisoning la intoxicación
  alimenticia

foot el pie
for: for me para mí
  what for? ¿para qué?
  for a week (para) una semana
foreigner el extranjero
  (*female*) la extranjera
forest el bosque
  (*tropical*) la selva
forget olvidar
fork el tenedor
fountain pen la (pluma) estilográfica
fourth cuarto
France Francia
free (*not engaged*) libre
  (*no charge*) gratis
freezer el congelador
French francés
french fries las patatas fritas
friend el amigo
  (*female*) la amiga
friendly simpático
front: in front of ... delante de ...
frost la escarcha
fruit la fruta
fruit juice el zumo de frutas
fry freír
frying pan la sartén
full lleno
  I'm full (*up*) estoy lleno
full board pensión completa
funny divertido
  (*odd*) raro
furniture los muebles

garage (*for parking*) el garage
garbage la basura
garbage can el cubo de la basura
garbage can liner la bolsa de basura
garden el jardín
garlic el ajo
gas la gasolina
gas station la gasolinera
gas-permeable lenses las lentes de contacto semi-rígidas

gate la puerta
  (*at airport*) la puerta de embarque
gay (*homosexual*) gay
gear shift la palanca de velocidades
gel (*hair*) el gel
German alemán
Germany Alemania
get (*fetch*) traer
  have you got ...? ¿tiene ...?
  to get the train coger el tren
get back: we get back tomorrow nos volvemos mañana
  to get something back recobrar algo
get in (*of train, etc.*) subirse
  (*of person*) llegar
get off (*bus, etc.*) bajarse
get on (*bus, etc.*) subirse
get out bajarse
  (*bring out*) sacar
get up (*rise*) levantarse
Gibraltar Gibraltar
gift el regalo
gin la ginebra
ginger (*spice*) el jengibre
girl la chica
girlfriend la novia
give dar
glad alegre
glass (*material*) el cristal
  (*for drinking*) el vaso
glasses las gafas
glossy prints las copias con brillo
gloves los guantes
glue el pegamento
go ir
gold el oro
good bueno
  good! ¡bien!
goodbye adiós
government el gobierno
granddaughter la nieta
grandfather el abuelo
grandmother la abuela
grandparents los abuelos
grandson el nieto

grapes las uvas
grass la hierba
gray gris
Great Britain Gran Bretaña
green verde
grocer's la tienda de comestibles
groundcloth la lona impermeable
ground floor la planta baja
guarantee (noun) la garantía
  (verb) garantizar
guide el/la guía
guide book la guía turística
guitar la guitarra
gun (rifle) la escopeta
  (pistol) la pistola

hair el pelo
haircut el corte de pelo
hair dryer el secador (de pelo)
hair salon la peluquería
hairspray la laca
half medio
  half an hour media hora
half board media pensión
ham el jamón
hamburger la hamburguesa
hammer el martillo
hand la mano
handbrake el freno de mano
handle (door) el picaporte
handsome guapo
hangover la resaca
happy contento
harbor el puerto
hard duro
  (difficult) difícil
hardware store la ferretería
hat el sombrero
  (woollen) el gorro
have tener
  I don't have … no tengo …
  do you have …? ¿tiene …?
  I have to go tengo que irme
  can I have …? ¿me da …?

hay fever la fiebre del heno
he él
head la cabeza
headache el dolor de cabeza
hear oír
hearing aid el audífono
heart el corazón
hearts (cards) corazones
heater la estufa
heating la calefacción
heavy pesado
heel el talón
  (shoe) el tacón
hello hola
  (on phone) dígame
help (noun) la ayuda
  (verb) ayudar
hepatitis la hepatitis
her: **it's for her** es para ella
  give it to her déselo
  her book su libro
  her shoes sus zapatos
  it's hers es suyo
high alto
highway la autopista
hill el monte
him: **it's for him** es para él
  give it to him déselo
hire alquilar
his: **his book** su libro
  his shoes sus zapatos
  it's his es suyo
history la historia
hitchhike hacer auto-stop
HIV positive seropositivo
hobby el hobby
home: **at home** en casa
homeopathy la homeopatía
honest honrado
  (sincere) sincero
honey la miel
honeymoon el viaje de novios
hood (car) el capó
horn (car) el claxon
  (animal) el cuerno

horrible horrible
hospital el hospital
hour la hora
house la casa
hovercraft el aerodeslizador
how? ¿cómo?
hungry: I'm hungry tengo hambre
hurry: I'm in a hurry tengo prisa
husband el marido
hydrofoil la hidroaleta

I yo
ice el hielo
ice cream el helado
ice skates los patines para hielo
if si
ignition el encendido
immediately inmediatamente
impossible imposible
in en
  in English en inglés
  in the hotel en el hotel
  in Barcelona en Barcelona
  he's not in no está
inexpensive barato
infection la infección
information la información
inhaler *(for asthma, etc.)* el spray,
  el inhalador
injection la inyección
injury la herida
ink la tinta
inn la fonda
inner tube la cámara (neumática)
insect el insecto
insect repellent la loción anti-mosquitos
insomnia el insomnio
instant coffee el café instantáneo
insurance el seguro
interesting interesante
internet el internet
interpret interpretar
interpreter el/la intérprete
invitation la invitación

Ireland Irlanda
Irish irlandés
Irishman el irlandés
Irishwoman la irlandesa
iron *(material)* el hierro
  (for clothes) la plancha
  (verb) planchar
is es/está
island la isla
it lo/la
Italian *(adj.)* italiano
Italy Italia
its su

jacket la chaqueta
jam la mermelada
jazz el jazz
jeans los tejanos, los vaqueros
jellyfish la medusa
jeweler's la joyería
job el trabajo
jog *(verb)* hacer footing
jogging suit el chandal
joke la broma
  (story) el chiste
just *(only)* sólo
  it's just arrived
  acaba de llegar

kettle el hervidor de agua
key la llave
kidney el riñón
kilo el kilo
kilometer el kilómetro
kitchen la cocina
knee la rodilla
knife el cuchillo
knit hacer punto
knitwear artículos de punto
know saber
  (person, place) conocer
  I don't know no sé

label la etiqueta
lace el encaje
laces *(shoe)* los cordones (de los zapatos)
lady la señora
lake el lago
lamb el cordero
lamp la lámpara
lampshade la pantalla
land *(noun)* la tierra
    (verb) aterrizar
language el idioma
large grande
last *(final)* último
    last week la semana pasada
    at last! ¡por fin!
late: it's getting late se está haciendo tarde
    the bus is late el autobús se ha
retrasado
later más tarde
laugh reír
Laundromat la lavandería automática
laundry *(dirty)* la ropa sucia
    (washed) la colada
laundry detergent el detergente
laxative el laxante
lazy perezoso
leaf la hoja
leaflet el folleto
learn aprender
leather el cuero
left *(not right)* izquierdo
    there's nothing left no queda nada
leg la pierna
lemon el limón
lemonade la limonada
length la longitud
lens la lente
less menos
lesson la clase
letter *(mail)* la carta
    (of alphabet) la letra
letter carrier el cartero
lettuce la lechuga
library la biblioteca
license el permiso

license plate la matrícula
life la vida
light *(noun)* la luz
    (adj.: not heavy) ligero
    (not dark) claro
light bulb la bombilla
lighter el encendedor
lighter fuel el gas para el encendedor
light meter el fotómetro
like: I like it me gusta
    I like swimming me gusta nadar
    it's like … es como …
    like this one como éste
lime *(fruit)* la lima
line *(noun)* la cola
    (verb) hacer cola
lipstick la barra de labios
liqueur el licor
list la lista
liter el litro
litter la basura
little *(small)* pequeño
    it's a little big es un poco grande
    just a little sólo un poquito
liver el hígado
lobster la langosta
lollipop el chupa-chups
long largo
lost and found office la oficina de
    objetos perdidos
lot: a lot mucho
loud alto
lounge *(in house)* el cuarto de estar
    (in hotel, etc.) el salón
lounge chair la tumbona
love *(noun)* el amor
    (verb) querer
    I love Spain me encanta España
lover el/la amante
low bajo
luck la suerte
    good luck! ¡suerte!
luggage el equipaje
luggage rack la rejilla de equipajes
lunch la comida

mad loco
magazine la revista
mail el correo
mailbox el buzón
Majorca Mallorca
make hacer
make-up el maquillaje
man el hombre
manager el/la gerente
  (hotel: male) el director
  (female) la directora
many: not many no muchos
map el mapa
  a map of Madrid un plano de Madrid
marble el mármol
margarine la margarina
market el mercado
marmalade la mermelada de naranja
married casado
mascara el rímel
mass *(church)* la misa
match *(light)* la cerilla
  (sport) el partido
material *(cloth)* la tela
matter: it doesn't matter no importa
mattress el colchón
maybe quizás
me: it's for me es para mí
  give it to me démelo
meal la comida
mean: what does this mean?
  ¿qué significa esto?
meat la carne
mechanic el mecánico
medicine la medicina
Mediterranean el Mediterráneo
medium *(sherry)* amontillado
medium-dry *(wine)* semi-seco
meeting la reunión
melon el melón
menu la carta
  fixed-price menu el menú (del día)
message el recado
middle: in the middle en el centro
midnight medianoche

milk la leche
mine: it's mine es mío
mineral water el agua mineral
minute el minuto
mirror el espejo
Miss Señorita
mistake la equivocación
mobile phone el teléfono móvil
modem el modem
mom mamá
money el dinero
month el mes
monument el monumento
moon la luna
moped el ciclomotor
more más
morning la mañana
  in the morning por la mañana
Morocco Marruecos
mosaic el mosaico
mosquito el mosquito
mother la madre
motorboat la motora
motorcycle la motocicleta
mountain la montaña
mountain bike la bicicleta de montaña
mouse el ratón
mousse *(for hair)* espuma moldeadora
mouth la boca
move *(verb: something)* mover
  (oneself) moverse
  (house) mudarse (de casa)
  don't move! ¡no se mueva!
movie la película
Mr. Señor
Mrs. Señora
much: much better mucho mejor
  much slower mucho más despacio
mug la jarrita
museum el museo
mushroom la seta
music la música
musical instrument el instrumento
  musical
musician el músico

mussels los mejillones
must: I must … tengo que …
mustache el bigote
mustard la mostaza
my: my book mi libro
  my keys mis llaves

nail (*metal*) el clavo
  (*finger*) la uña
nail clippers el cortauñas
nailfile la lima de uñas
nail polish el esmalte de uñas
name el nombre
  what's your name? ¿cómo se llama usted?
napkin la servilleta
narrow estrecho
near: near the door junto a la puerta
  near New York cerca de New York
necessary necesario
neck el cuello
necklace el collar
need (*verb*) necesitar
  I need … necesito …
  there's no need no hace falta
needle la aguja
negative (*photo*) el negativo
neither: neither of them
  ninguno de ellos
  neither … nor … ni … ni …
nephew el sobrino
never nunca
new nuevo
news las noticias
newspaper el periódico
newsstand el kiosko de periódicos
New Zealand Nueva Zelanda
New Zealander
  (*man*) el neozelandés
  (*woman*) la neozelandesa
  (*adj.*) neozelandés
next siguiente
  next week la semana que viene
  what next? ¿y ahora qué?

nice bonito
  (*pleasant*) agradable
  (*to eat*) bueno
niece la sobrina
night la noche
nightclub la discoteca
nightgown el camisón
night porter el vigilante nocturno
no (*response*) no
  I have no money no tengo dinero
nobody nadie
noisy ruidoso
noon mediodía
north el norte
Northern Ireland Irlanda del Norte
nose la nariz
not no
  he's not … no es/está …
notebook el cuaderno
nothing nada
novel la novela
now ahora
nowhere en ninguna parte
nudist el/la nudista
number el número
nut (*fruit*) la nuez
  (*for bolt*) la tuerca

oars los remos
occasionally de vez en cuando
occupied ocupado
octopus el pulpo
of de
office (*place*) la oficina
  (*room*) el despacho
often a menudo
oil el aceite
ointment la pomada
OK vale
old viejo
  how old are you? ¿cuántos años tiene?
olive la aceituna
olive oil el aceite de oliva
olive tree el olivo

omelette la tortilla
on ... en ...
one uno
onion la cebolla
only sólo
open (adj.) abierto
  (verb) abrir
operation la operación
operator la operadora
opposite: opposite the hotel enfrente
  del hotel
optician el oculista
or o
orange (fruit) la naranja
  (color) naranja
orange juice el zumo de naranja
orchestra la orquesta
ordinary corriente
organ (music) el órgano
other: the other (one) el otro
our nuestro
  it's ours es nuestro
out: he's out no está
outside fuera
oven el horno
over ... encima de ...
  (more than) más de ...
  it's over the road está al otro lado
  de la calle
  when the party is over
  cuando termine la fiesta
  over there allí
oyster la ostra

package (parcel) el paquete
packet el paquete
  (cigarettes) la cajetilla
  (candy, chips) la bolsa
padlock el candado
page la página
pain el dolor
paint (noun) la pintura
pair el par
pajamas el pijama

palace el palacio
pale pálido
pancakes las crepes
pants los pantalones
pantyhose los pantis
paper el papel
  (newspaper) el periódico
paraffin la parafina
parcel el paquete
pardon? ¿cómo dice?
parents los padres
park (noun) el parque
  (verb) aparcar
parking lights las luces de posición
parsley el perejil
part (hair) la raya
party (celebration) la fiesta
  (group) el grupo
  (political) el partido
pass (in car) adelantar
passenger el pasajero
passport el pasaporte
pasta la pasta
path el camino
pay pagar
peach el melocotón
peanuts los cacahuetes
pear la pera
pearl la perla
peas los guisantes
pedestrian el peatón
pen la pluma
pen pal el amigo por correspondencia
  (female) la amiga por correspondencia
pencil el lápiz
pencil sharpener el sacapuntas
people la gente
pepper la pimienta
  (red, green) el pimiento
peppermints las pastillas de menta
per: per night por noche
perfect perfecto
perfume el perfume
perhaps quizás
perm la permanente

petticoat la combinacíion
pharmacy la farmacia
phone book la guía telefónica
phone booth la cabina telefónica
phonecard la tarjeta telefónica
photocopier la fotocopiadora
photograph *(noun)* la foto(grafía)
  (verb) fotografiar
photographer el fotógrafo
phrase book el libro de frases
piano el piano
pickpocket el carterista
picnic el picnic
piece el pedazo
pill la pastilla
pillow la almohada
pilot el piloto
pin el alfiler
  (clothes) la pinza
pine *(tree)* el pino
pineapple la piña
pink rosa
pipe *(for smoking)* la pipa
  (for water) la tubería
piston el pistón
pizza la pizza
place el lugar
  at your place en su casa
plant la planta
plastic el plástico
plastic bag la bolsa de plástico
plastic wrap el plástico para envolver
plate el plato
platform el andén
play *(theater)* la obra de teatro
  (verb) jugar
please por favor
plug *(electrical)* el enchufe
  (sink) el tapón
pocket el bolsillo
pocketbook el bolso
pocketknife la navaja
poison el veneno
police la policía
police officer el policía

police station la comisaría
politics la política
poor pobre
  (bad quality) malo
pop music la música pop
pork la carne de cerdo
port *(harbor)* el puerto
  (drink) el oporto
porter *(hotel)* el conserje
Portugal Portugal
Portuguese portugués
possible posible
post *(noun)* el correo
  (verb) echar al correo
postcard la postal
poster el póster
post office (la oficina de) Correos
potato la patata
potato chips las patatas fritas
poultry las aves
pound *(money)* la libra
  (weight) la libra
powder el polvo
  (make up) los polvos
prawns las gambas
prefer preferir
prescription la receta
pretty bonito
  (quite) bastante
priest el cura
private privado
problem el problema
protection factor (SPF) el factor de
  protección
public público
pull tirar de
puncture el pinchazo
purple morado
purse el monedero
push empujar
put poner
Pyrenees los Pirineos

quality la calidad
quarter un cuarto
question la pregunta
quick rápido
quiet tranquilo
  (person) callado
quite *(fairly)* bastante
  (fully) completamente

radiator el radiador
radio la radio
radish el rábano
railroad el ferrocarril
rain la lluvia
rain boots las botas de agua
raincoat la gabardina
raisins las pasas
raspberry la frambuesa
rare *(uncommon)* raro
  (steak) poco pasado
rat la rata
razor blades las cuchillas de afeitar
read leer
reading lamp el flexo
  (bedside) la lamparilla de noche
ready listo
receipt el recibo
receptionist el/la recepcionista
record *(music)* el disco
  (sport, etc.) el récord
record player el tocadiscos
record store la tienda de discos
red rojo
  (wine) tinto
refreshments los refrescos
refrigerator el frigorífico
relative el pariente
relax relajarse
  (rest) descansar
religion la religión
remember: I remember me acuerdo
 I don't remember no me acuerdo
rent *(verb)* alquilar
reservation la reserva

rest *(noun: remainder)* el resto
  (verb: relax) descansar
restaurant el restaurante
restaurant car el vagón-restaurante
restroom *(men)* los servicios de caballeros
  (women) los servicios de señoras
return *(come back)* volver
  (give back) devolver
return ticket el billete de ida y vuelta
rice el arroz
rich rico
right *(correct)* correcto
  (not left) derecho
ring *(wedding, etc.)* el anillo
ripe maduro
river el río
road la carretera
rock *(stone)* la roca
  (music) el rock
roll *(bread)* el bollo
roof el tejado
room la habitación
  (space) sitio
rope la cuerda
rose la rosa
round *(circular)* redondo
 it's my round me toca a mí
row *(verb)* remar
rowboat la barca de remos
rubber *(material)* la goma
rubber band la goma
ruby *(stone)* el rubí
rug *(mat)* la alfombra
  (blanket) la manta
ruins las ruinas
ruler *(for drawing)* la regla
rum el ron
run *(verb)* correr
runway la pista

sad triste
safe *(not dangerous)* seguro
safety pin el imperdible

sailboard la tabla de windsurfing
sailboat el balandro
salad la ensalada
sale *(at reduced prices)* las rebajas
salmon el salmón
salt la sal
same: the same dress el mismo vestido
  the same people la misma gente
  same again, please lo mismo otra vez,
  por favor
sand la arena
sandals las sandalias
sand dunes las dunas
sandwich el bocadillo
sanitary napkins las compresas
sauce la salsa
saucepan el cazo
sauna la sauna
sausage la salchicha
say decir
  what did you say? ¿qué ha dicho?
  how do you say …? ¿cómo se dice …?
scampi las gambas
scarf la bufanda
  (head) el pañuelo
school la escuela
scissors las tijeras
Scotland Escocia
Scotsman el escocés
Scotswoman la escocesa
Scottish escocés
screw el tornillo
screwdriver el destornillador
sea el mar
seafood mariscos
seat el asiento
seat belt el cinturón de seguridad
second el segundo
second floor el primer piso
see ver
  I can't see no veo
  I see comprendo
sell vender
separate *(adj.)* distinto
separated separado

serious serio
several varios
sew coser
shampoo el champú
shave *(noun)* un afeitado
  to have a shave afeitarse
shaving foam la espuma de
  afeitar
shawl el chal
she ella
sheet la sábana
  (of paper) la hoja
shell la concha
shellfish mariscos
sherry el jerez
ship el barco
shirt la camisa
shoelaces los cordones de los zapatos
shoe polish la crema de zapatos
shoes los zapatos
shop la tienda
shopping la compra
  to go shopping ir de compras
short corto
shorts los pantalones cortos
shoulder el hombro
shower *(bath)* la ducha
  (rain) el chaparrón
shower gel el gel de ducha
shrimp las quisquillas
shutter *(camera)* el obturador
  (window) el postigo
sick: I feel sick tengo náuseas
  to be sick *(vomit)* devolver
side *(edge)* el borde
sidewalk la acera
sights: the sights of … los lugares
  de interés de …
silk la seda
silver *(metal)* la plata
  (color) plateado
simple sencillo
sing cantar
single *(one)* único
  (unmarried) soltero

single room la habitación individual
sister la hermana
skid patinar
skiing: to go skiing ir a esquiar
skin cleanser la leche limpiadora
ski resort la estación de esquí
skirt la falda
skis los esquís
sky el cielo
sleep *(noun)* el sueño
  (verb) dormir
sleeper el coche-cama
sleeping bag el saco de dormir
sleeping pill el somnífero
slippers las zapatillas
slow lento
small pequeño
smell *(noun)* el olor
  (verb) oler
smile *(noun)* la sonrisa
  (verb) sonreír
smoke *(noun)* el humo
  (verb) fumar
snack la comida ligera
sneakers los zapatos de deporte
snow la nieve
so: so good tan bueno
  not so much no tanto
soaking solution *(for contact lenses)*
  la solución limpiadora
soap el jabón
soccer el fútbol
soccer ball el balón
socks los calcetines
soda water la soda
somebody alguien
somehow de algún modo
something algo
sometimes a veces
somewhere en alguna parte
son el hijo
song la canción
sorry ¡perdón!
  I'm sorry perdón/lo siento
  sorry? *(pardon)* ¿cómo dice?

soup la sopa
south el sur
South America Sudamérica
souvenir el recuerdo
spade la pala
spades *(cards)* picas
Spain España
Spaniard *(man)* el español
  (woman) la española
Spanish español
  the Spanish los españoles
speak hablar
  do you speak …? ¿habla …?
  I don't speak … no hablo …
speed la velocidad
speed limit el límite de velocidad
spider la araña
spinach las espinacas
spoon la cuchara
spring *(mechanical)* el muelle
  (season) la primavera
square *(noun: in town)* la plaza
  (adj.) cuadrado
staircase la escalera
stairs las escaleras
stamp el sello
stapler la grapadora
star la estrella
start *(noun: beginning)* el principio
  (verb) empezar
station la estación
statue la estatua
steak el filete
steal robar
  it's been stolen lo han robado
steamer *(boat)* el vapor
stockings las medias
stomach el estómago
stomachache el dolor de
  estómago
stop *(noun: bus)* la parada
  (verb) parar
  stop! ¡alto!
storm la tormenta
strawberries las fresas

stream *(small river)* el arroyo
street la calle
string la cuerda
stroller la sillita de ruedas
strong fuerte
student el/la estudiante
stupid estúpido
suburbs las afueras
subway el metro
sugar el azúcar
suit *(noun)* el traje
  it suits you te sienta bien
suitcase la maleta
sun el sol
sunbathe tomar el sol
sunburn la quemadura de sol
sunglasses las gafas de sol
sunny: it's sunny hace sol
sunshade la sombrilla
suntan: to get a suntan
  broncearse
suntan lotion la loción bronceadora
suntanned bronceado
supermarket el supermercado
supper la cena
supplement el suplemento
sure seguro
surname el apellido
sweat *(noun)* el sudor
  (verb) sudar
sweater el jersey
sweatshirt la sudadera
sweet *(adj.: not sour)* dulce
  (sherry) oloroso
swim *(verb)* nadar
swimming pool la piscina
swimming trunks el bañador
switch el interruptor
synagogue la sinagoga

table la mesa
take tomar
take off el despegue
talcum powder los polvos de talco

talk *(noun)* la charla
  (verb) hablar
tall alto
tampons los tampones
tangerine la mandarina
tapestry el tapiz
tea el té
teacher el profesor
  (female) la profesora
telephone *(noun)* el teléfono
  (verb) llamar por teléfono
television la televisión
temperature la temperatura
  (fever) la fiebre
tent la tienda (de campaña)
tent pole el mástil
tent stake la estaquilla, la estaca
than que
thank *(verb)* agradecer
  thank you gracias
  thanks gracias
that: that one ése/ésa
  that bus ese autobús
  that man ese hombre
  that woman esa mujer
  what's that? ¿qué es eso?
  I think that ... creo que ...
the el/la
  (plural) los/las *(see p 5)*
their: their room su habitación
  their books sus libros
  it's theirs es suyo
them: it's for them es para ellos/ellas
  give it to them déselo
then entonces
  (after) después
there allí
  there is/are ... hay ...
  is/are there ...? ¿hay ...?
these: these men estos hombres
  these women estas mujeres
  these are mine éstos son míos
they ellos/ellas
thick grueso
thin delgado

think pensar
  I think so creo que sí
  I'll think about it lo pensaré
third tercero
thirsty: I'm thirsty tengo sed
this: this one éste/ésta
  this man este hombre
  this woman esta mujer
  what's this? ¿qué es esto?
  this is Mr. … éste es el señor …
those: those men esos hombres
  those women esas mujeres
throat la garganta
through por
thumbtack la chincheta
thunderstorm la tormenta
ticket (train, etc.) el billete
  (theater, etc.) la entrada
ticket office la taquilla
tide la marea
tie (noun) la corbata
  (verb) atar
tight ajustado
time tiempo
  what's the time? ¿qué hora es?
timetable el horario
tin hojalata
tip (money) la propina
  (end) la punta
tire el neumático
tired cansado
tissues los pañuelos de papel
to: to America a América
  to the station a la estación
  to the doctor al médico
toast la tostada
tobacco el tabaco
today hoy
together juntos
toilet (in a house) el baño
  (in public establishment) los servicos
toilet paper el papel higiénico
tomato el tomate
tomato juice el zumo de tomate
tomorrow mañana

tongue la lengua
tonic la tónica
tonight esta noche
too (also) también
  (excessively) demasiado
tooth el diente
  back tooth la muela
toothache el dolor de muelas
toothbrush el cepillo de dientes
toothpaste la pasta dentífrica
tour la excursión
tourist el/la turista
tourist office la oficina de turismo
towel la toalla
tower la torre
town la ciudad
town hall el ayuntamiento
toy el juguete
tractor el tractor
tradition la tradición
traffic el tráfico
traffic jam el atasco
traffic lights el semáforo
trailer la caravana, el remolque
train el tren
translate traducir
translator el traductor
  (female) la traductora
travel agency la agencia de viajes
traveler's check el cheque de viaje
tray la bandeja
tree el árbol
trip el viaje
truck el camión
true cierto
  it's true es verdad
try intentar
tunnel el túnel
tweezers las pinzas
typewriter la máquina de escribir

umbrella el paraguas
uncle el tío
under … debajo de …

underpants los calzoncillos
undershirt la camiseta
understand entender
  I don't understand no entiendo
underwear la ropa interior
United States Estados Unidos
university la universidad
unleaded sin plomo
until hasta
unusual poco común
up arriba
  (*upward*) hacia arriba
urgent urgente
us: it's for us es para nosotros/nosotras
  give it to us dénoslo
use (*noun*) el uso
  (*verb*) usar
  it's no use no sirve de nada
useful útil
usual corriente
usually en general

vacancies (*rooms*) habitaciones libres
vacation las vacaciones
vacuum cleaner la aspiradora
valley el valle
valve la válvula
vanilla la vainilla
vase el jarrón
veal la (carne de) ternera
vegetables la verdura
vegetarian vegetariano
vehicle el vehículo
very muy
  very much mucho
video (*tape*) la cinta de vídeo
  (*film*) el vídeo
video recorder el (aparato de) vídeo
view la vista
viewfinder el visor de imagen
villa el chalet
village el pueblo
vinegar el vinagre
violin el violín

visit (*noun*) la visita
  (*verb*) visitar
visitor el/la visitante
vitamin pills las vitaminas
vodka el vodka
voice la voz

wait esperar
  wait! ¡espere!
waiter el camarero
  waiter! ¡camarero!
waiting room la sala de espera
waitress la camarera
  waitress! ¡Oiga, por favor!
Wales Gales
walk (*noun: stroll*) el paseo
  (*verb*) andar
  to go for a walk ir de paseo
wall la pared
  (*outside*) el muro
wallet la cartera
war la guerra
wardrobe el armario
warm caliente
  (*weather*) caluroso
was estaba/era
washing machine la zapatilla
wasp la avispa
watch (*noun*) el reloj
  (*verb*) mirar
water el agua
waterfall la cascada
water heater el calentador (de agua)
wave (*noun*) la ola
  (*verb*) agitar
wavy (*hair*) ondulado
we nosotros/nosotras
weather el tiempo
website la web site, el sitio web
wedding la boda
week la semana
welcome (*verb*) dar la bienvenida
  you're welcome no hay de qué
Welsh galés

Welshman el galés
Welshwoman la galesa
were: we were éramos/estábamos
  you were era/estaba
  (familiar) eras/estabas
  they were eran/estaban
west el oeste
wet mojado
what? ¿qué?
wheel la rueda
wheelchair la silla de ruedas
when? ¿cuándo?
where? ¿dónde?
whether si
which? ¿cuál?
whiskey el whisky
white blanco
who? ¿quién?
why? ¿por qué?
wide ancho
  3 meters wide de tres metros de
  anchura
wife la mujer
wind el viento
window la ventana
wine el vino
wine merchant el vinatero
wing el ala
with con
without sin
woman la mujer
wood *(material)* la madera
wool la lana

word la palabra
work *(noun)* el trabajo
  (verb) trabajar
worse peor
worst (el) peor
wrapping paper el papel de envolver
  (for presents) el papel de regalo
wrench la llave inglesa
wrist la muñeca
writing paper el papel de escribir
wrong equivocado

year el año
yellow amarillo
yes sí
yesterday ayer
yet todavía
  not yet todavía no
yogurt el yogur
you usted
  (familiar) tú
your: your book su libro
  (familiar) tu libro
  your shoes sus zapatos
  (familiar) tus zapatos
yours: is this yours? ¿es suyo esto?
  (familiar) ¿es tuyo esto?
youth hostel el albergue juvenil

zipper la cremallera
zoo el zoo